House Beautiful
WINDOW
WORKSHOP

House Beautiful

WINDOW
WORKSHOP

TESSA EVELEGH

HEARST BOOKS

A Division of Sterling Publishing Co., Inc.

Created, edited, and designed by
Duncan Baird Publishers Ltd, Castle House,
75–76 Wells Street, London W1T 3QH

Managing editor: Emma Callery
Designer: Alison Shackleton
Illustrations: Kate Simunek

Photographs: see credits on page 160. The publisher has made
every effort to properly credit the photographers whose work
appears in this book. Please let us know if an error has been made,
and we will make any necessary changes in subsequent printings.

Library of Congress Cataloging-in-Publication Data
Evelegh, Tessa.
  House beautiful window workshop / Tessa Evelegh.
    p. cm.
  ISBN 1-58816-362-8
  1. Draperies. 2. Window shades. 3. Draperies in
interior decoration. I. Title: Window
  workshop. II. House beautiful. III. Title.
TT390.E295 2004
747'.3--dc22

2003056985

10 9 8 7 6 5 4 3 2

Published by Hearst Books
A Division of Sterling Publishing Co., Inc.
387 Park Avenue South, New York, NY 10016

House Beautiful is a trademark owned by Hearst Magazines
Property, Inc., in USA, and Hearst Communications, Inc., in
Canada. Hearst Books is a trademark owned by Hearst
Communications, Inc.

www.housebeautiful.com

Distributed in Canada by Sterling Publishing
c/o Canadian Manda Group, 165 Dufferin Street,
Toronto, Ontario, Canada M6K 3H6

Distributed in Australia by Capricorn Link
(Australia) Pty. Ltd.
P. O. Box 704, Windsor, NSW 2756 Australia

Printed in China
ISBN 1-58816-362-8

CONTENTS

FOREWORD

The range of window treatment choices can be dazzling these days, and in editing House Beautiful, I'm continually inundated with new and exciting ideas from designers, makers, and manufacturers so we can offer our readers the very best of the latest solutions. And that's not so difficult when I have between one and two hundred pages in which to indulge myself every month; but when it comes to choosing window treatments for our own home, both my wife, Monica, and I know it comes down to a lot of thought, research, visualization, and planning. The very latest trend is not necessarily the right answer in every situation. I always love to start by imagining how the windows might have been treated when the house was new—how they were influenced by the fashions and tastes of the time, by the circumstances of the family that may have lived there, and, in the case of old houses, even by the lack of central heating and air conditioning.

This visualization, along with the architecture of the windows, can have a surprising influence on our end choices. But first, Monica and I always think carefully about our lifestyle and how we use each room, and, indeed, how we might be using it in five years' time. With the experience of raising two kids to college age, I know that, by then, my younger daughters, now aged eight and one, will have very different needs (and, indeed, their own ideas), so we have decided to concentrate on cheap and cheerful in their rooms for the time being.

Being more advanced in years, Monica and I have a much stronger sense of our own style, so we can afford to invest more on the living room windows. Changing the use of a room can have a dramatic bearing on window choices, too. The feminine drapes in the spare bedroom just won't work when we turn it

into a home office. Shades will be more practical, but first, we're going to keep a diary of where the sun is at different times of the day to help us decide whether we want pull-up, pull-down, Venetian, or vertical slats. The color choice will probably be the last decision that we have to make. I have always believed in spending the time to work out what's right for us in our particular situation. And given the same time, same family, and same tastes, we could always come up with very different solutions if we lived in a different house.

That is what Window Workshop is all about. It doesn't dictate a particular style; rather, it is a guidebook to working out what is right for you in your home. Whether you love lavish traditional drapes, or whether you prefer a clean, minimal look, this book will take you step by step through the process of creating successful window treatments. Starting out by helping you to assess the architecture of your windows, it guides you through the maze of all the different traditional and modern curtain styles and shades that range from the frankly feminine Austrian to a choice of state-of-the-art climate controllers. Over 200 color photographs offer plenty of window inspiration; and informative illustrated sections show the range of choices in rods, headings, tassels, trims, and tiebacks. There is help at hand when it comes to buying fabrics and choosing colors, and there's a clearly illustrated guide to measuring. Broken down into bite-sized nuggets of information that will not become dated, quick and easy to assimilate, Window Workshop promises to be my curtain companion for the foreseeable future.

MARK MAYFIELD
Editor in Chief, House Beautiful

SCENE
SETTING

DAYLIGHT FROM DAWN TO DUSK

Homes bathed in natural daylight lift the spirits, bringing a sense of well-being that can never be matched by the flick of a switch. When light is limited, we can become melancholy; and in northern countries, some people even suffer from the aptly named SAD (seasonal affective disorder), a recognized form of depression linked with long, dark winter nights.

The intensity of natural daylight is astounding. On a cloudy day, the light outside is one hundred times more powerful than an electric light inside; and on a sunny day, it is one thousand times more powerful. Little wonder, then, that bringing natural daylight into homes for as much of the day as possible has been a priority of architects down the centuries.

However, not all natural light is necessarily desirable. The glare of direct sunlight can be as uncomfortable as the lack of light can be depressing. So when planning window treatments, be aware of the sun's position at different times of the day and build in flexibility to suit the use of the room. For example, you may want to have plenty

▶ **Light fantastic**

Where the view is wonderful and there are no close neighbors, there's no reason why you shouldn't go for maximum natural light. Glare spots can be dealt with by using carefully positioned ceiling-hung panels.

▼ **Subtle shade**

Early-morning light is not a problem in this bedroom; but, by noon, the sun is dazzling through the top of the window. The short valance-style sheers behind the Roman shades cut the glare when the shades are open. At night, the main shades are let down to block out all light.

of natural daylight in your home office, but find that glare at some times of the day competes with the computer screen. The solution could be a series of shades or shutters with adjustable louvers that can be opened and closed during the day as the light moves across the sky. If glare coming through the top of the windows is a problem, use shades that can be lowered, such as roller and Roman. Where natural light is at a premium at all times of the day, consider installing shades that pull up from the windowsill, rather than down from the top of the frame.

While heavy drapes and valances block out a larger proportion of the natural daylight than less voluptuous shades, this need not always be the case. If you love the look of drapes but also want maximum daylight, hang them from extra-long curtain rods that allow the curtains to be opened clear of the architrave (molding around the window). Where glare is a problem, team drapes with shades that can be pulled down partly when the sun's rays prove just a little too bright.

▲ **Light all around**

Double-aspect windows make this an extremely light and airy room, and as the owners place high priority on natural light they have opted for fine white pleated shades with which to dress them. The beauty of these shades is that they can be lowered just as far as needed, whatever the time of day.

▲ Fully adjustable

Shutters with adjustable louvers are the best means of controlling the amount of light. As the sun moves, the louvers can be opened and closed in turn to cut out the glare, or let in maximum daylight. Since they can be adjusted to any angle, they are equally effective, whatever the time of day.

◄ Light shade

It is the afternoon sun that shines into this smart white bedroom, and the owners enjoy the dawn, so a light London shade is all that is needed to dress the window.

WINDOW ARCHITECTURE

The first step to planning a window treatment that suits your home is to assess the architecture of the window itself. However much you adore elegant traditional swags and tails, they will never look right if you have a cozy cottage or a modern home built to different proportions. Building fashions have changed and developed over the centuries and decades; and while windows have not necessarily always been standardized, there are recognizable styles, which were complemented by particular curtain styles. Of course, their historical significance can be a good starting point for window treatments, but there is no reason why they shouldn't be adapted to suit current fashions.

Casement
Almost any style of window décor can be used on these outward-opening windows (here seen from the outside). Cut the drapes to sill or floor length; either looks good.

Georgian sash
These windows included shutters, but swags and tails were often used too. Today, their beautiful proportions mean you can use almost any treatment, even simple sheer panels.

French doors
For inward-opening doors, install shades on the frame, or install drapes on a hinged rod. Outward-opening doors suit curtain rails and rods, and shades can be mounted above.

Loft style

Original loft homes were abandoned or converted warehouses with large metal-framed windows. Pared back, this style is best suited to shades or simple panels.

Victorian bay

These are usually tall with sash windows. Modern bays are generally made up of casement windows. Treat the whole bay as a single unit (see page 144).

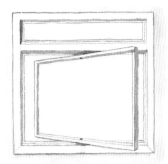

Pivot

If pivoting windows are to be used regularly, attach shades directly to the frame. If they are left closed, however, treat them to suit their proportions.

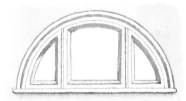

Semicircular or round

These pretty windows are usually set high in the room to provide light. If possible, leave them as they are or fit sandblasted glass for privacy.

Arched windows

These elegant windows are usually a feature of the room. Beautiful if unadorned, they also look wonderful fitted with custom-made shutters or pull-up shades (see also page 140).

WINDOWS IN CONTEXT

The architectural style of windows may suggest different treatments, but it is not until you look at the window in the context of the room and its use that you can really begin to plan. Yes, conventional wisdom may suggest that, generally, swags and tails look magnificent with tall, elegant, Georgian-style architecture and not so good on tiny cottage windows, but there is no rigid dictum. For a general guideline, however, it is best to start by assessing the architecture. Are the windows so beautifully proportioned that you want to show them off with a minimal solution, or do their proportions need a little help from valances or cornice boxes? Look at how the windows are arranged within the room. Are they arranged in a bay or in pairs? Are they tall or short? Are they set high or low? Are they recessed or flush? Do they have windowsills, shutters, or neither? Next, think of your own style. The answer to all these questions will

▶▲ Elaborate bay
It would be a shame not to show off the exquisite architecture of this bay. Beautiful arched windows have been offset by elaborate plasterwork on the cornice and pillars, which provides a perfect framework. As this house has no immediate neighbors, there is no urgent need for privacy, and even the most discreet of shades would have covered up the elegant arches.

▶ Cottage charm
Old cottages built for cold climates very often have thick walls and small windows to conserve heat, but the result is dark rooms. The solution here has been to use a sheer fabric that filters the light.

▶▶ Minimal cover
Well-proportioned Georgian-style windows like this one look good dressed in any style. Here, a minimal Roman shade, set between the architraves, lends a dressed look, while showing off the beauty of the window architecture.

▲ Shutter style

Highly practical shutters fold back neatly during the day to display pretty windows, while offering total privacy at night when they're shut. They can be closed in turn on each of the three aspects to shut out any of the sun's glare.

▲ Tall order

Elaborate drapes and swags would have shrouded this pair of tall, narrow Georgian-style windows. The matching Austrian shades with tails in pure silk provide a neater solution, yet team with the traditional style of the room.

help you decide on a window treatment—one that is simple, or one that is more elaborate.

You will also need to decide on a style that is appropriate for the use of the room. For example, a minimal solution that may look marvelous in a living room that does not need privacy could be most unsuitable for bedrooms or bathrooms, which need more privacy. Likewise, elaborate drapes and valances can look wonderful in sitting rooms, but rarely in kitchens, where they will not only seem fussy, but all too soon look less than gorgeous as they collect grease and dust. Smart shades, on the other hand, can look modern, workmanlike, and sleek in the busiest of kitchens.

▲ Shapely show off
It would have been a shame to spoil the elegant lines of this window, so the curtain rod has been set below the curved top, and the drapes dress only the rectangular part.

◄ Bay solution
Installing rods around a curve often presents problems, and the resulting drapes can all too easily overwhelm handsome architecture. Shades, such as these pretty sheer ones with their harlequin edging, can be an ideal solution as they fit within the architrave of each window.

FABRIC CHOICES

Unlike upholstery materials, which are necessarily heavyweight, curtain fabrics can range from the thick and sumptuous to gauzy fine. Gathered treatments hang best when made in dense, lined, and interlined fabrics, while simple modern panels can look wonderful in translucent, diaphanous fabrics, such as organdy, loose-weave linen, or fine-cotton voiles. The style of your home will help you to decide whether you wish to go for rich drapes in elegant silks, velvets, or brocades, or a simpler country look in a cotton weave or print. You may prefer to experiment with exotic ethnic prints, such as batiks or ikats, which come in very bright color

▲ Fine choice

Diaphanous colored sheers make glorious modern panels that protect your privacy without cutting down on the light. When buying, feel the drape—firmer sheers, such as organdy or loose-weave linen, work best, but almost any sheer will do. If in doubt, hold it up to check how it falls.

▶ Bold print

Printed fabrics are an ideal way to bring bold pattern and color to a room. Strong designs, like this one, work best when used flat, such as on this Roman shade.

combinations and, not being fashion-based, stand the test of time.

Whatever you choose, don't be hurried into expensive mistakes. When making your selection, bear in mind the drape of the fabric and how it will be used. Hold it up in the way it will hang—flat or gathered. Silks, taffetas, dupions, linens, and linen mixes (a linen/cotton combination) all drape well when they are gathered; Roman shades work best in heavier fabrics, such as linens. Cotton is a relatively inexpensive choice and comes in a huge variety of patterns and colors, and linings and interlinings can make up for weight where it is needed.

Take home a selection of swatches to see how the colors and designs work together in your room. Once you're happy with a particular combination, order a larger swatch of each fabric—say ¼ yard. Pleat up those that will be gathered, and then pin all the elements into position around the window. Leave the swatches there for several days to see how they look as the light changes; make sure you check them out in day and night light. Only when you're totally delighted should you place the order.

►▲ Feminine touch

Simple geometric cotton weaves always look good on windows; search out household linen departments where there's a wide choice of tea towels and tablecloths that can be transformed into shades or even drapes. Adding a deep lace edging turns the purely practical into the decidedly pretty.

► Smart combination

Team the gorgeous with the prosaic for smart effect. Here, a bottom border of bold ticking brings a modern touch to the rich pink dupion.

►► Gingham style

A favorite fabric for country-style curtains, the regular checks of gingham work well either flat or gathered, as demonstrated by this London shade.

FABRIC CHOICES: color

We all have our favorite colors, and, though it might sound obvious, this is always the best place to start. It is easy to be swayed by fashion or simply by the idea that you want something different. But if you've always found plum depressing, that's not going to change simply because it's in vogue. You also need to discount all the conventional wisdom such as "blue is a cold color," which immediately wipes out a large section of the spectrum. If ice blue looks chilly in your north-facing living room, try a warmer shade, such as lavender, or team it with a hot color, such as raspberry. The key is in how you put colors together. One trick is to think in terms of types of color scheme, such as neutral, bright, warm, and so on (see right), and then try out several different colors within that "family."

Color effects

◆ **Take inspiration for** color combinations from the fabrics. If one incorporates several different hues, use these as cues for a color scheme.

◆ **You can be daring** with accent colors. These are like seasoning in cooking as they set off the main ingredients, but a little goes a long way. So, for example, you may love the combination of blue and aqua. With some tiny added touches of something stronger, such as lime green or navy blue, you'll create quite a different look.

◆ **Light affects color**, so take large swatches home to try in the room, and see how they look at different times of the day.

◆ **Seasons affect colors** and mood, so beware of choosing fabrics in midwinter when you'll be more inclined toward deep colors that might look rather depressing at other times of the year.

◆ **If in doubt**, choose curtain fabrics that are a little lighter than the wall colors. In that way, the windows will give the impression of being a light source, even at night, when the drapes are pulled together or the shades pulled down.

SWATCH WATCH

Putting together interesting color combinations is much easier if you think of color groupings, rather than the individual hues. Look at the ideas below and develop them to suit your own tastes.

Neutrals

Whites, creams, and neutrals always look elegant and sit happily together. Team cream with taupe, café au lait, and sand, or tiny touches of color for accent.

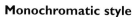

Monochromatic style

Any scheme that consists of one hue plus white or black is monochromatic. China blue and white is a classic example. For added drama, team tones of the same color with black.

Pastel combinations

Easy-to-live-with sugar-almond shades work well in monochromatic schemes, or as several different colors linked by similar tones.

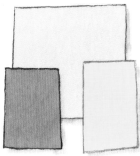

Light and shade

By keeping to a color family, but using contrasting tones, you can create interesting light and shade effects. Here, light aqua is contrasted with deep aquamarine. The lime accent lends spark to the overall scheme.

Hot pink curtains become a focal point when set against cream walls.

Vibrant orange trims transformed pink curtains into an extrovert element of the room. This brave combination works because of its boldness and because the two colors are similar in tone.

Lime green, used as an accent, adds zing to the scheme, while accentuating the heat of the main colors.

◀ **A splash of color**

Some of the most successful color combinations are those that go against the traditional preconceptions of color wisdom. For example, orange and pink are often seen as "clashing," yet here they make a vibrant mix as the orange trim lends spark to the pink drapes, resulting in a confident combination.

FABRIC CHOICES: pattern

Pattern behaves differently at the window than it does elsewhere. Large designs are distorted, and sometimes lost, in the folds of traditional drapes; when Roman shades are drawn up, dramatic motifs can be cut off in an unflattering way. Use the guidelines given on these pages to help you successfully use patterned fabrics for window treatments.

Looking at fabrics in the store will give you only a hint of how they will look at home. You'll need to think about how the pattern will look with the curtains open and closed, or when the shade is drawn up and let down. Also consider the scale of the pattern. Will it overwhelm the window? Or will it be too subtle when seen from a distance? If so, could you add emphasis with trims, an interesting heading, or inspired tiebacks?

Pattern effects

◆ **From a distance,** fine-line stripes tend to look more pastel than broader bands of color.

◆ **Checks with several** colors can provide an excellent starting point for a scheme if you choose colors to decorate your room that match the different hues in the fabric.

◆ **Coordinate floral patterns** with stripes for a smart look, or for fresh country appeal use ginghams, checks, or spots.

◆ **The effect of** allover patterns is to break up the color so that it becomes softer, especially when viewed from a distance. For added interest, set allover prints against plains.

◆ **Teamed with bold,** coordinating patterns, small motifs can look like an allover design. If such patterns are combined with matching plains in a room that is otherwise decorated in a restrained way, they add points of interest.

◆ **Allover patterns** don't benefit from being crowded by other patterns or distorted by gathers. So show them off at their best by using the fabric for flat panels or on shades.

SWATCH WATCH

How much pattern you have in the room is really a style decision, but here are some guidelines to help you make the coordination work well.

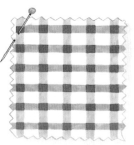

Stripes and ticking

Such simplicity combines well with both pretty country florals and city-smart plains.

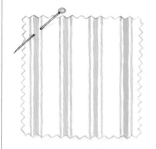

Checks

Checks are more casual than stripes. They look good with florals, and ginghams introduce a country feel.

Florals

Scale is important with floral patterns. Look at full-blown roses for generous drapes, and sprigs for small curtains.

Allover prints

Spots, dots, or squiggles, and repetitive designs, such as toile de Jouy, can look textured from a distance.

Small motifs

Neat motifs—from tiny rosebuds to diminutive ducks on children's fabrics —are truly versatile.

Bold motifs

Whether you choose large, painterly florals or bold abstracts, these motifs always make a statement.

Patterns of different scales team better than same-size patterns, which tend to compete with each other.

The drapes and valance set the scene in this bedroom, and all else fits in around them. Several different designs can sit happily together if they are linked by a single color.

▲ Mix 'n' match

This pretty blue-and-white bedroom incorporates several different patterns to great effect, yet manages to retain a fresh and open feel.

A tiny, allover wallpaper pattern gives the impression of textured pale blue paint from the distance, and so avoids "fighting" with the fabric design.

FABRIC CHOICES: texture

If pattern is not your style, you can bring interest to the windows with texture. Monochromatic schemes can look very smart with the introduction of surface variety. Luscious velvets or chenille drapes look wonderful set against fine translucent sheers; full homespun hessian curtains take on a luxurious feel when trimmed with deep velvet ribbon; smooth silk drapes can be enhanced by lacy panel sheers; even embroidered fabrics provide a texture of their own.

Trims are another way to add texture. Shiny glass beads bring sparkle to matte fabrics; fabulous fringes can set off smooth fabrics, such as finely woven linens. Paler color schemes, such as white or cream, look especially good when texture is introduced because these shades are more light reflective than darker ones.

Texture effects

◆ **The way you** use fabric can affect the overall appearance of texture. For example, although a fine linen provides smart, flat contrast against other textures, when gathered, it can create a completely new texture in its own right.

◆ **Too many different** textures will look disorderly. Just one in contrast to the rest of the interior is usually enough. If in doubt, try to keep to a maximum of three different textures.

◆ **Look out for** interesting new textures on woven fabrics, made possible by modern technology.

◆ **Texture brings elegant** interest to pattern-free schemes. Just the addition of a trim, such as a fringe, tassel, or sparkling glass beads, could be all you need.

◆ **Paler color schemes, such** as whites, creams, and neutrals, tend to set off textures best. This is because they are more light reflective.

Italian stringing creates particularly elegant draping to enhance the texture created by the folds.

The shiny silk content of the velvet helps accentuate the contrast between the light and shade created by the folds.

A lacy panel brings a contrast to the deep pile velvet. Used flat, this adds to the effect.

Smooth cotton cushions introduce a third texture, making even greater play on the textural qualities of this room.

◀ Three in one

Three different textures add subtle interest to a yellow monochromatic scheme. By choosing velvet for the drapes, opening them and drawing them becomes a daily pleasure. A pretty lacy panel not only keeps the room private, but provides a soft contrast against the sharp dogtooth edging of the curtains.

SWATCH WATCH

Even small touches of textural variety add interest to a room, especially if you love elegant neutral schemes.

Chunky weaves

For something striking, use heavy weaves, such as ticking, hessian, or cotton dobby.

Cool linen

Fine and crisp, white linen is the perfect choice for setting off any other texture.

Rich velvet

Highly tactile, velvet or silk catches the light, enhancing the gathers on drapes.

Embroidery

Silken threads on linen or thick crewel wools on heavier fabrics add texture.

Soft chenille

A modern favorite, chenille brings a softness that's irresistible to the touch.

Sparkling detail

Fine, smooth organdy is set off against bright, sparkly glass beads.

WINDOW
STYLES &
MOODS

WINDOW STYLES & MOODS
FINDING YOUR STYLE

For most of us, our sense of style is an ongoing process that continues to develop throughout our lives. Our ideas change according to our needs at the time, the style of our house, interior fashions, and what we may have inherited from previous homes. Few of us can afford to throw everything out and start again, and, indeed, that's not always desirable. The most appealing homes are those that show the patina of time—possessions that have been collected over the years; colors that have come together by accident, sometimes to stunning effect. So where do you begin?

The easiest first step is to decide what sort of person you are. Do you love collecting and displaying things, or do you prefer a clean surface, a minimal look that's quick to wipe down? Are you a free-standing furniture person, or is built-in more your style? The answers to these two questions will point you in a generally traditional or modern direction. Even if you prefer a traditional look, there is still

▶ **Swedish simplicity**
Unpretentious rod-hung, gathered curtains are the ideal solution for the traditional Swedish style. Pale fabrics in cream, white, aqua, or celandine green work well with this light and airy style.

▼ **Open contemporary**
An uncluttered look teamed with pale shades is a favorite contemporary style. Elegant neutral shades are the perfect complement—they're not overly fussy yet lend a soft and feminine look to the whole interior.

plenty of room to develop your style. For example, while polished wood furniture was the fashion in the sixties, and stripped pine in the seventies, the vogue has moved on to painted traditional French- or Swedish-style furniture, and all this has a bearing on which window treatments you choose.

Collecting inspiration from books, magazines, and real homes is one of the first steps to take in developing your own style. What do you really like? Whether you veer toward the traditional or the contemporary, the following pages provide some starter inspiration packed with the best window treatments and ideas for each style.

◄ Clutter-free shutters

If you find voluptuous folds of fabric too fussy for your taste, go for an architectural solution and install shutters.

▼ Traditional elegance

Teamed with a London shade that can be pulled down as dusk falls, these refined Empire-style silk drapes with elegant Italian stringing can remain drawn back at all times.

WINDOW STYLES

opulent

colonial

simple

traditional

sleek

classic

lavish

eclectic

elaborate

country

relaxed

PERIOD OPULENCE

Elaborate curtain styles date back to the late eighteenth century, at the start of the Regency period when interior decorating was a new profession. Inspired by the exquisite proportions of Georgian houses and the beautiful clothes of the period, they dressed windows in elegant swathes of silks and satins and trimmed them with generous fringes, tassels, ribbons, and rosettes. This was the era when swags and tails were born.

These traditional styles still work well when used in larger rooms with tall windows. If you love the look, but live in a more modest house, pare it down by using just one swag instead of several, and choose simpler trimmings. Length is the key when planning an opulent setting, so always aim for elegant, full-length floor-to-ceiling drapes.

Inspired solutions

◆ **This style relies** on fabrics that drape elegantly. Look for flowing silks and satins that have the body to support the folds in the fabric without looking heavy.

◆ **Elaborate curtains look** best in plain colors. Line them in a flattering contrast to show off the reverse on the swags.

◆ **New trims, such** as fun bobbles made in extroverted colors, can be used to update the style.

▼ Period colors

The tall windows of period houses can take dramatic colors, such as this acid yellow. The pretty pink ribbons tied into Maltese-cross rosettes soften the overall effect, lending a delightfully feminine feel.

▼ Dramatic drapes

Generous swags are a hallmark of period opulence, so show them off using fabric that both drapes well and reflects the light, such as this silk in sage green.

Wide enough to take three swags, this window is also tall enough to retain an elegant look. The tails are lined in the same yellow as the inner curtains.

Deep fringing emphasizes the swags and tails, while rope braid enhances the generously draped fabric.

COLONIAL STYLE

The unpretentious Colonial style of early America, which eighteenth-century settlers brought across the Atlantic from Europe, continues to have much appeal. The pared-back look of simple polished furniture and homespun woven fabrics, born of a rigorous life with little time for fancy frills or swags, translates nowadays into relaxed family living.

Curtains are simply gathered and hung from a rod; shades are Roman or London, rather than fabric-greedy Austrian. Simple lace panels and lightly gathered sheer valances are also in keeping with the Colonial look, and can be used to add a softer touch.

Inspired solutions

◆ **Look for woven** cotton fabrics in checks or vertical stripes and make them into simple gathered curtains for a country look, or into basic shades for city style— either solution is acceptable when planning a Colonial-type window dressing.

◆ **Favorite colors are** inspired by nature: blues, greens, and sunshine yellows, as well as earthy shades such as oxblood and yellow ocher. This was because only natural dyes were originally available. By using these colors as inspiration, you'll be able to create a more authentic look.

◆ **Avoid valances, swags**, tiebacks, and elaborate trims, but add interest with contrast linings to suit your style.

◆ **Add detail with** interesting finials that would have been available during the Colonial period, such as wrought-iron balls, arrows, and shepherd's crooks.

▲ **Homespun solutions**
Woven cotton fabrics in checks and stripes were a Colonial favorite. Far too down-to-earth to be flounced and frilled, they nevertheless look welcoming made into gathered curtains on a simple wooden rod.

▶ **Inspired solutions**
This shade is the perfect treatment as the window is tall and narrow, and drapes would have made the window look even narrower while blocking out some of the light.

The cornice box doubles up as a valance, providing a neat, streamlined solution that sets off a well-proportioned sash window.

Smart, striped fabric makes an unpretentious London shade—the perfect halfway solution between formal city-smart and ostentatious Austrian.

Matching shades, upholstery, and seat cushions keep the overall look clean and simple.

TRADITIONAL COUNTRY

Relaxed and pretty, country style has universal appeal because it is inspired by all things natural. Traditionally, the fabrics used for this style of window dressing are woven from natural fibers, such as cottons, linens, and soft wools, often incorporating simple geometrics such as ginghams, checks, and stripes. Printed designs take reference from the country and are usually pretty florals, leaves, or country animals or scenes.

The fresh, easy-to-live-with colors are based on natural dyes—china blues and denims, soft rose pinks, sunny yellows, and clear spring greens.

Traditional country style also features flamboyant floral fabrics that are sometimes teamed with matching or coordinating wallpapers. In addition, ginghams of all sizes, generally in red or yellow, are frequently major players for window dressings.

Inspired solutions

◆ **Gathered curtains** in fresh, pretty cottons are typical country style. There's a huge, inexpensive selection available—but wash the curtains before putting them up to ensure they are preshrunk.

◆ **Don't scrimp on** fabric or the effect will look cheap. Line the curtains so they hang better.

◆ **Wooden curtain rods** with simple traditional finials work well in a country setting. Alternatively, if you like the look of metal, choose traditional blacksmith-style wrought iron.

◆ **Soft valances are** effective too. They can be used to adjust visually the proportions of the windows.

◆ **Tiebacks, rather than** more architectural holdbacks, lend a soft country look.

▶ **Floral favorite**
Pretty rose-pink floral cotton is the perfect choice for country-style gathered drapes. Teamed with a generous valance, they make a delightful framing for the French doors opening onto the veranda.

Roses, a favorite country icon, feature strongly on this fresh cotton print. The allover design works well with gathered curtains as it is not lost in the folds and has been used on the headboard too as a unifying element.

Tassel braiding trims the valance (and echoes in the bed valance) while enhancing the fabric colors. This is further emphasized by the long key tassels.

A softly shaped valance is typical of traditional country style for a fresh and feminine effect.

▲ Gingham style

Gingham, especially if it is red or yellow, is a hallmark of traditional country style. Used both for window treatments and for upholstery, it creates a fresh, relaxed feel. Here, made into Roman shades, it offers a neat country-style solution for the bay window.

The window is the guideline for the length of country curtains. Generally, they would be cut to windowsill length, but here they hang to the floor because they frame French doors.

ECLECTIC

If we're honest, there's a bit of the eclectic in all of us. Who can afford to discard everything as style fashions change? And who would want to? A well-put-together eclectic look is the hallmark of style confidence. It is usually developed over time, retaining favorite possessions and adding new finds in a way that results in a cohesive overall look. The skill is to have a sure sense of style that transcends the junk shop look. Here are some key points to consider.

Try to keep to one kind of wood for furniture. For example, polished mahogany does not sit well with pine, though cream-painted can work well with either. Disparate pieces can also be given unity by a coat of paint in the same color.

Think about scale, too. Generously proportioned pieces will diminish the dainty in large spaces and dominate in small spaces. Pieces in proportion to the room work well together.

You can really make the eclectic style work for you when it comes to window treatments. Instead of sticking slavishly to a whole room style, take elements and adapt them to suit the situation.

Inspired solutions

◆ **Use window treatments** to link elements within the room. One of the easiest ways to make the link is by color, so you could choose a fabric in the same shade as the upholstery, but create a style that suits the window proportions.

◆ **Where an elaborate** window style would be more in keeping with the furnishings, in eclectic rooms you can simplify the treatment to create some balance in the setting.

◆ **Eclectic can allow** you to adapt curtains in a stylish way when moving to a new house, as old curtains can be given extra length in a contrast fabric that teams with any new furniture you might have acquired.

◆ **Alternatively, give old** drapes new trims to link them to new furniture.

▲ Ancient meets modern

The uncompromisingly modern steel four-poster bed is teamed here with an antique French mahogany table. Both pieces are strong and the window treatments could have gone in either direction. The neat pull-up shades in royal blue both match the bed and open up a small window to offer a streamlined solution, with a fresh, airy feel.

▲ Soften the bold

The bold, chunky shapes of twentieth-century furniture could have been an incongruous choice for this fine nineteenth-century Paris apartment with its intricate plasterwork detailing, had not the drapes provided the perfect link. French-pleated and hung on a dark wood rod, they're softer than the plain shades that are normally associated with the furniture style.

Instead of elaborate swags and tails, often associated with the Empire style, the drapes have been simply gathered onto a rod. This works well here as the window is not very tall and swags would have made them look squat.

The choice of a modern red-and-white striped silk fabric is a clever one because it alludes to the popularity of stripes during the Empire period. However, the finer stripes are more modern and work well in a room of these proportions.

The curtains are cut extra long to make the window appear taller and add a luxurious feel.

◀ **Stylish combination**

This room, painted yellow and featuring a large circular table and bold golden eagle, has strong Empire styling, but the window treatment has a modern look.

CLASSIC MODERN

Tasteful, elegant, and restrained, classic modern was the style of the late twentieth century and continues to be popular. It is an international look that pares down the fussiness of traditional drapes, but retains a coziness that can be lost in more modern interiors. Curtains are usually gathered and hung on wooden curtain rods with much of the detailing in the pleating—pencil pleats, French pleats, goblet, or puffball (see pages 74–75). Valances, if there are any, are generally tailored, rather than flounced, and trims are discreet. Creams and neutrals are favorite shades because they work well with both dark and light furniture; they do not become dated and can take subtle changes with the addition of taupe, coffee, and sand.

Highly patterned fabrics generally look a little fussy with classic modern styling, but with the advent of modern technology, and the availability of a wide range of new woven fabrics, texture has become more important in the lexicon of window dressing.

Inspired solutions

◆ **Choose plain fabrics** or those with a patterned weave, such as damasks in floral or leafy designs, or add interest with texture.

◆ **If you'd like** to add pattern, choose a geometric such as subtle checks or stripes, either as a print, or a textured weave. Jacquards with a tiny motif set against a plain background can work well, too.

◆ **For the perfect** classic modern setting, choose full-length rather than sill-length curtains.

◆ **Tailored Roman** or roller shades work well with classic modern styles.

▶ **Coffee and cream**
Classic is restrained, not plain. Here, a cream scheme has been given interest with coffee-colored panels on either side of each drape.

Hang drapes from a wooden curtain rod with wooden rings. Add detail with interesting wooden finials.

Coffee-colored borders define each curtain, and bring elegant interest to the cream fabric.

French pleats create full, well-spaced folds that hang well, especially if the curtains have been lined and interlined.

To add height to the windows and to create a sense of luxury, cut drapes full length so they touch the ground, if not puddle onto it.

▲ Feminine charm

Classic modern does not necessarily mean unadorned. Here, delicately patterned ivory curtains are given a soft, feminine touch with frills on the inside edges. The tailored valances, trimmed with fine coffee-colored braid, introduce height and elegance to the French doors.

MAXIMUM IMPACT

Create maximum impact at the window by making a loud statement using color or pattern. This is a modern look that does not sit happily with fine antique furniture, but spells confidence in the right setting. The key is to be bold with the fabrics, but to keep the overall treatment simple, free from too much fussy detailing. You also need to bear in mind that since the window is the source of natural light, you'll need to steer clear of fabrics that might be too dark and heavy, which would have a detrimental effect.

Conversely, the impact may be watered down if the fabric is too translucent. The colors in sheer fabrics, especially, can be diminished by strong light coming through them. When choosing fabric, take it to a window or door and hold it up to check how the color is affected by natural light.

This kind of brave decorating needs absolute confidence to be successful, so before you make your final decision for your fabric, buy a large enough sample to incorporate the whole pattern and hang it at your own window for a few days until you're absolutely sure it will work.

Inspired solutions

◆ **If you choose** a large pattern, check that the size of the window allows for pleasing repeats.
◆ **For maximum impact** with flair, choose brighter rather than darker colors.
◆ **If you want** to create a link with dark colors in the rest of the décor, do this with smart trims or window-frame paint, rather than overwhelming expanses of dark fabric that cut out the light.

▶ **Bold mix**
Even a relatively narrow strip of fabric for a valance can look terrific if it is used effectively. Here, the bold yellow and purple colors in the material have been bravely echoed in the décor, to striking effect.

The softly gathered curtains continue the color and the theme without reducing the impact of the valance.

The valance has been cut to a depth that centers on the bold medallion motif. It has been used flat, rather than gathered, to create maximum impact.

▲ Clever contrast

The combination of black and white creates the ultimate contrast and ultimate impact. To keep the window décor light, the curtains are white and simply linked to the scheme by black trims. The black window frames continue the theme.

▲ Color impact

Here, the diaphanous sheer curtains in orange and red zing out as a focal point in a mainly white room. They work because, being translucent, they don't prevent the light from pouring into the room.

MODERN COUNTRY

The country look is a perennial favorite, and, taking the same basic principles, each generation has its own interpretation. Natural fabrics, such as cottons, linens, and wool, remain essential to a genuine country style; and the patterns still tend to be simple geometric weaves, such as checks and stripes alongside printed florals. The difference, however, lies in the scale of the motifs and how the patterns are put together.

In previous decades, florals were often flamboyant, featuring full-blown roses, and trails of wisteria and honeysuckle; in the twenty-first century, they are more likely to be tiny rosebuds set against a background of pin dots or hairline-fine stripes. Furthermore, in times past, patterned fabrics were often matched or coordinated with wallpaper. Instead, modern country favors plain painted walls combined with simple shades or curtains with tab or tie tops.

Inspired solutions

◆ For tab- or tie-topped curtains, choose pure cottons in simple geometrics or small florals.
◆ Hang curtains on wooden or metal rods with pretty finials, such as shepherd's crooks or twists.
◆ Roman shades made from cottons or antique linen tea towels lend a smart country look.
◆ Modern country curtains are softly gathered rather than fully pleated.
◆ Search out pretty trims, such as beads or fun fringing, or bobbles, to stitch to drape edges.
◆ Tiebacks are simple—a string of glass beads; a ribbon or braid tie.

▼ **Fresh checks**
Geometric weaves are a popular country choice as the color is broken up and the pattern is not too fussy.

A white-painted rod keeps the window treatment light. Wrought-iron, stainless steel, and nickel rods would also be appropriate for the modern country look, as long as the finials are pretty and feminine, rather than pared back and sleek.

The tab-topped curtain is not gathered, just cut a little too wide for the window to retain a sense of movement.

The modern country look is based on simplicity. The translucent pure cotton fabric is not lined and interlined, so the look remains fresh and pretty.

◄ **All is calm**

Light and feminine are the hallmarks of modern country, and here the off-white painted furniture, walls, and window treatment are broken up by blue-and-white checks in a range of sizes.

WINDOW MOODS

light

fresh

sunny

feminine

warm

cozy

natural

romantic

modern

bright

airy

LIGHT & AIRY

Rooms that are bathed in natural light lift the spirits and bring a sense of joy and well-being. Whether you prefer to live with a sleek, modern look, or to be surrounded by something a little more traditional, the key to creating or enhancing a light and airy room lies in how you dress the windows.

The demand for natural light has transformed contemporary interior design, moving the emphasis from traditional coziness to a brighter, more open feel. Furthermore, central heating and double glazing have liberated us from a need to conserve warmth using heavy drapes to pull together against cold winter nights. So now, even those people living in chilly northern climates can enjoy the light and airy look.

Inspired solutions

◆ **Show off the** window architecture. Simply avoid shrouding the window with pelmets, valances, and swags and tails, all of which disguise windows and block out light.

◆ **Choose fabric colors** from the paler end of the spectrum. Even if you paint your walls with stronger tones, cream or pastel colors at the window will reflect light into the room.

◆ **Gather curtains less,** rather than more, to lend a lighter look. Simple panels in a crisp fabric look fabulous with no gathers at all.

◆ **Translucent sheer fabrics** are a fail-safe way to create a light and airy feel. For a smart interior, choose a firm sheer with body and drape, such as pure cotton organdy. This fabric always retains its crispness, even after laundering.

▶ **Sheer delight**
The most up-to-date sheer panels complement the exquisite Regency-style windows. The panels allow plenty of natural light to flood into this elegant and classic interior throughout the day.

Three brass bosses act as minimal fixings and holdbacks. They reflect the light and shun even a hint of fussiness.

The valances and panels have been made from the same striped sheer fabric. But it has been cut so the panels have horizontal stripes and the valances vertical ones to add interest to the window treatment.

▲ Feminine floatiness

Light and pretty valances can work well with the airy look—so long as they don't shroud the windows and block out the light. Here, curtains made of a light glazed cotton in pale cream (that is lighter than the walls) are complemented by the prettiest of petal-edged valances to lend an airy feel to an otherwise traditional room.

▲ Modern winner

Nothing could be easier than dressing a window with ready-made, tab-topped, sheer curtains; yet they are soft and restrained, and perfect for any modern interior, as they allow maximum light to stream through the windows.

SUNNY & BRIGHT

Colors at the hot end of the color spectrum—red, orange, and yellow—generally add a bright and sunny feel to interiors, and have always been popular in both warm climates and cool. In hot countries, such as Mexico and India, home owners have never been afraid of mixing clashing colors, such as orange with fuchsia, and yellow with pink, to stunning effect; while more conservative cold-country dwellers have preferred to be more understated, choosing buttery yellows, soft apricots, and delicate pinks.

Whatever tones you choose from the red-orange-yellow palette, the effect is going to be one of sunny warmth. Further enhance a bright and welcoming atmosphere by choosing light window treatments that shun heavy drapes and valances.

Inspired solutions

◆ **Choose curtain rods** or wires and simple tab or tie tops. Unfussy roller, Roman, and tie-up shades in sunny-colored fabrics also enhance the look.

◆ **Choose simple headings,** and hang curtains on painted or stained wooden curtain rods.

◆ **Keep shades simple.** Roman and roller shades are ideal as they fit neatly within the architraves.

◆ **Choose lighter and** brighter shades of the hot colors for a sunny look all year.

▲ **Sunny days**
The yellow fabric of these simple pencil-pleat drapes hung full length in a white room lends a sunny feel on even the dullest of days. The simple styling throughout the living room keeps the mood light and bright.

▲ **Maximum sunshine**
The combination of tangerine walls and yellow gingham shades creates a warm ambience. The unlined Roman shade allows light to filter through, creating a yellow cast that complements the sunny feel.

A goblet heading adds interest to the top of the drapes, yet produces large, loose folds for a contemporary look.

White curtains make for a light window treatment and allow maximum daylight into the room.

Full-length curtains offer a contemporary look, so let them fall to the floor, even if the windowsill is considerably higher.

◀ Plain and simple

The bright and sunny look is essentially contemporary, so an unpretentious window treatment that combines an interesting goblet heading with simple cream curtains is the perfect solution.

WARM & COZY

In centuries past, long, cold winters created a need for warm and cozy rooms that conserved the heat both by providing insulation and by stopping the drafts. Window treatments had a major part to play in this as full-length drapes that were lined and interlined provided efficient insulation, while valances, and swags and tails cut out the drafts.

Alongside the practicalities of keeping out the cold, decorating in warm colors created a feeling of coziness, even before the fires were lit. Although central heating and double glazing have reduced the need for warm window treatments, the intimate mood is still beguiling with its welcoming ambience.

Inspired solutions

◆ **Choose deep-toned** colors from the warm end of the spectrum, such as rich plums and wines, earthy shades, and burnt orange.

◆ **Lush floor-length** drapes that are lined and then interlined exclude drafts and enhance the warmth. If your windows are of the right proportions, add a valance or swags and tails for further insulation.

◆ **Choose luxurious fabrics** that have rich piles, such as velvets and chenilles. Other dense-weave fabrics work well too, including jacquards, damasks, and dupions. Any of these fabrics are guaranteed to make you feel warm and comfortable.

▶ **Completely cosseted**

Full drapes with deep valances in warm burnt orange are very snug in this smart bedroom.

▶▶ **Plum choice**

Rich mulberry shades are a classic choice for the cozy look and can still look pretty, especially if lightened with a sunny shade, such as buttery yellow. These full-length drapes were made to twice the width of the window to ensure full gathers, which provide excellent insulation and also look great.

Drapes that reach right down to the floor ensure that all potential drafts are kept well at bay.

Drapes are fully gathered, lined, and interlined to keep out the cold.

The background color of the curtain fabric is matched to the walls. The pattern is then broken up by a lighter yellow pattern, so that at night, when the drapes are drawn, the windows continue to give the impression of being a light source.

EASY LIVING

Modern life leaves many of us with little time to fuss over perfection. We want to be able to relax without having to worry about whether our furnishings are going to be spoiled by spills or the rigors of day-to-day family life. We can do without the stress of keeping up the standards of a perfectly tidy show home.

This does not mean that we don't care about the look of our home, or that we are limited to a choice of "sensible" dark colors or patterns that won't show the marks. The key is to aim for a casual look and factor in for easy laundering.

Your choice of window treatment has a great bearing on the easy-living look. Keep curtains casual, both to make machine washing possible and to create a stylish, easy-going look. Aim for drapes with the most straightforward of headings (see pages 74 and 80) or use any of the structured shades described on pages 114–15. These are all easy to wipe clean. If you prefer softer shades, roller, Roman, and Swedish are the simplest stylistically—and to maintain (see pages 118–19).

Inspired solutions

◆ **Avoid formal valances**, tiebacks, or unnecessary trims. All these elements hinder laundering and complicate the look.

◆ **If you need** tiebacks, choose a simple ribbon or braid that can be knotted into position.

◆ **Choose curtain fabric** in any color you like—as long as it is easy to launder.

◆ **Avoid linings and** interlinings as these can so easily become tangled in the wash.

◆ **Textured fabrics look** smart and they also need minimal ironing.

▶ **A neutral position**
Simple cream cotton drapes, hooked onto curtain rings, take on an appealing look, setting the scene for an easy-living yet stylish sitting room, decorated in neutral shades.

A wooden rod and rings create a simple look that's conducive to easy living.

Avoid unnecessary trims, frills, and tiebacks that would complicate the finished effect.

Ungathered curtains both ease the laundry load and look less formal. Choose a fabric that drapes well to create a languorous look.

▲ Easy tie

Pretty lacy panels hung on simple curtain rods fixed inside the architraves make for a delightful, relaxed window treatment. During the day, a cream ribbon that is loosely tied around the middle of each drape allows the sunshine to stream in.

▲ Eclectic mix

Mixing antique and junk shop finds can be complemented by window treatments that don't try too hard. Here, plain cream curtains have been tied to a rod and topped with a simple valance.

ROMANTIC

Delicate, pretty, and yet free from unnecessary fuss, the romantic look depends largely on fabric choices, which are truly varied. For the best effect, consider softly textured fabrics such as slubby cottons or fine muslins, or perhaps go the other way and look at super-smooth and sensuous satins and silks.

The romantic look has universal appeal, evoking an ambience of hedonistic self-indulgence. But avoid the temptation to overly fuss romantic rooms, at their windows in particular. Too many frills and flounces can become overbearing, especially if they are liberally scattered all around the room; think instead of a soft and pretty look that is essentially feminine. Gentle folds of fabric cascading to the floor convey the essence.

Inspired solutions

◆ **Pastel colors are** the perfect choice if you are seeking the romantic look. The palest pink is always successful when creating this sort of atmosphere, as are soft lavenders, aquamarines, and pistachio greens. Cream works very well, too.

◆ **Great swathes of** fabric look lavish, so cut curtain material overly long, letting the drapes fall to a puddle on the floor.

◆ **Choose pretty headings** that encourage fabric to drape languorously, rather than make it stand stiffly on formal pelmet boards (see page 104).

◆ **Add romantic details**, such as light-reflecting glass beads, tiny bows, or delicate fringing.

▲ Romantic simplicity

Delicate, cut-worked sheer panels, hung by tiny brass rings, make for a delightfully romantic, rustic window treatment. The shutters can be closed, or roller shade lowered, whenever there's a need for privacy.

▲ French romance

Palest pink and generously cut, these silken curtains lend classic Paris salon-style chic to an elegant room. The zigzag-cut valances with tiny golden tassels stitched to each point add to the romance.

Brass finials and rings that are set off by white rods give the impression of jewelry, dressing the window in a romantic mood.

Glazed cotton in sugar-almond pink, with a puffball heading, looks just like a dressy ball gown —pure romance.

▲ All dressed up

Generously gathered curtains have a dressed-up look that flatters this romantic room. The simple fabric design complements this ebullience, especially when combined with the ornate heading.

By only having one drape on each rod, sunlight is allowed to pour in during the day.

THE WELL-DRESSED WINDOW

THE WELL-DRESSED WINDOW
DRAPES OR SHADES?

Do you adore textiles—their colors and their textures, the way they drape, the way they feel? Or are you happier in a clean, clutter-free interior? Your response to these questions provides the key to your major window treatment decision—whether to use shades, or whether to drape. However, it won't provide the full answer. You might find textiles, and the infinite ways they can be combined at windows, irresistible, but this does not mean they are necessarily the best solution for all the windows in the house.

First, consider the architecture of the windows. Are they beautifully proportioned and would you love to show them off by choosing discreet shades, or are they frankly mismatched and incongruous within the room? Drapes, which generally cover the architraves, are the best way to adjust proportions visually. There are so many types

▲ Feminine charm
A delicate sheer panel makes the most feminine of drapes for a bedroom furnished in the simplest of styles. Its translucency lets maximum light into what could be a dark room, while the embroidered border adds texture and interest.

▶ The long run
Venetian shades always look smart, and especially so in a kitchen where countertops generally emphasize the horizontal. Here, since they run the full length they almost look like a wall, rather than a window treatment.

of valance to choose from, offering flexibility when it comes to the positioning of rods and rails.

The use of the room is another consideration. Elaborate drapes in a bathroom, for example, not only look inappropriate, but the folds in the fabric will also lose their shape and attract mold due to the condensation that tends to build up in such rooms. Wipe-clean shades, or simple drapes or panels, are far more practical.

You'll also want to think about the level of light that you need in the room. This is particularly important in workrooms, such as home offices, sewing areas, even kitchens. You might want maximum daylight, or you might want to cut down the glare of direct sunlight at certain times of the day. Generally, shades offer more flexibility for controlling light than drapes. In bedrooms, on the other hand, you may desire the more intimate ambience of filtered light, and so choose drapes or shades that reduce incoming daylight.

◀ Cream topping
Floor-to-ceiling cream curtains make an ideal solution for an elegant, classic sitting room. The puffball heading brings a witty modern touch.

▼ Natural shades
Split-cane roll-up shades enhance the natural charm of this relaxed summer room. Fitting neatly within the architraves, the shades successfully introduce an unpretentious outdoor feel to the overall style of the room.

TOPS & TAILS

lavish

generous

rich

ornate

gathers

swags

simple

tabs

ties

clips

ribbons

TRADITIONAL HEADINGS

Full, lavish drapes are the hallmark of traditional window treatments, and the key to that fullness lies largely in the choice of heading, as each one has its own yardage requirements (see pages 74–75). The heading also adds interest to the top of the drape, contributing to the overall look of the window treatment. Although the choice of heading is a key decision, it needs to be considered in combination with the fixings, because the same heading will look very different depending on the rail or rod on which it is hung. So how to decide?

The many combinations available mean you really can be individualistic, so here are some guidelines. First, consider proportions—a deep heading or a window treatment with a deep valance looks better on tall windows. When using valances or elaborate swags and tails that cover curtain tops, set this off with a simple but smart heading for the drapes, such as pencil pleats.

If you love the traditional look, but don't want to shroud the windows in too much fabric (a good plan, especially if you don't have very large windows), opt for an elegant heading, such as French or goblet pleats hung on a generously long curtain rod that allows the drapes to hang clear of the windows. By using a window treatment of this kind, you will let in maximum light and keep it in scale with the rest of the room.

◀ **Italian-strung drapes on a curved board**

This most elegant of traditional styles, emulating the Empire-line dress fashions of the early nineteenth century, looks best on tall, slim windows in well-proportioned rooms. Here, the curtains have a goblet heading to create an elegant finish that is complemented by Italian stringing, an "invisible" form of holdback. Attached to a curved board, it is not possible to draw these drapes, so add draw-down Roman shades for when you need privacy.

▶ **Simple elegance**

The key to curtain success is to think of headings in combination with the whole treatment. Smart Regency-style architraves set off these tall, elegant windows, so instead of covering them with an elaborate treatment, the drapes have been hung within them. Visually, the top of the architrave makes up part of the heading, so the fabric has been given an unpretentious pencil-pleated heading.

The drapes are simply hitched back during the day for an understated, elegant treatment.

With smart reeded architraves, a simple gathered heading is all that is needed for this pretty treatment.

TRADITIONAL HEADINGS: your choice

Of the many headings that are available, the most basic one is the standard gather (not illustrated), which is a narrow heading giving even gathers. Choosing a heading is largely a matter of personal style, but broadly speaking, it's best to think in terms of scale. Long drapes look better with deeper headings, such as a wide puffball, whereas shorter ones benefit from a narrower heading, such as standard gathering or smocking. Evenly spaced pleats work for most windows, while well-spaced pleats, such as French or goblet, are best on bigger windows.

Each type of heading has a different fabric width requirement, so choose the heading first. The fabric requirements shown here are estimates—you will find that commercial heading tapes are marked with their own particular fabric requirements.

Pencil pleats

The perfect choice for curtains that are complemented by a valance or a pelmet board. Fabric requirement: 2 × the curtain rod length.

Puffball

A witty heading created by adding a fold of fabric at the drape top, which, when gathered, results in a frothy puffball. Fabric requirement: 2 × the curtain rod length.

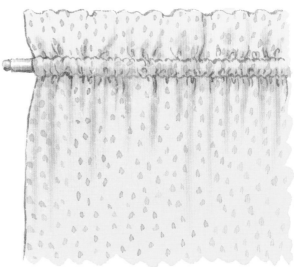

Slotted heading

An easy solution for lightweight bedroom curtains and nets. Fabric requirement: up to 3 × the curtain rod length —the lighter the fabric, the more you'll need.

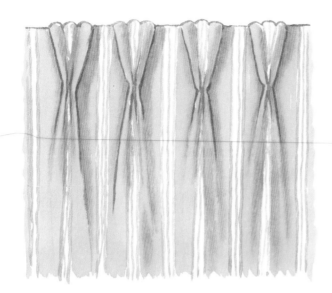

French or pinch pleats

An elegant, deep heading that looks good on longer curtains hung on a curtain rod. Fabric requirement: at least 2½ × the curtain rod length.

Goblet pleats

A more relaxed, feminine version of French pleats with gathered, rather than pleated, sections. Fabric requirement: 2½ × the curtain rod length.

Italian stringing

Attached to a curved board, these drapes are drawn and closed using a cord threaded through curtain rings sewn at the back. Fabric requirement: 2 × the curtain rod length.

Diamond smocked

Hand smocking, using transfer dots, is a pretty hand-sewn heading. It looks best where the detail can be seen. Fabric requirement: 2 × the curtain rod length.

TRADITIONAL DRAPES: style options

Traditional curtains need not mean old-fashioned styling. With the wide selection of gathered headings and valances at your fingertips (see pages 74 and 102) you can design window treatments to suit contemporary tastes. Make it work for you with fabric choices, heading detail, and smart or witty trims. Think of the window treatment as a whole, considering each element in combination.

DETAILS THAT COUNT

◆ **Fullness matters when** it comes to successful traditional window treatments. So, if your budget won't stretch, look for a better-value material rather than scrimping on yardage.

◆ **Allow for pattern** matching, especially if you choose a large design print. Estimate on one extra pattern repeat for each drop of fabric.

◆ **Use trims for** emphasis by picking out the background color of patterned fabrics or as a contrast to plains.

◆ **Valances alter window** proportions, so use this to your advantage. Install them well above the window to lend height, or team a lower fixing with a deep valance for a cozier feel.

◆ **Set off self-valances** with contrasting trims.

◆ **Use trims to** update existing drapes. The same plain curtains can take on very different personalities if they are given smart plain borders, flirty bobbles, tufts, or fringes.

Border trims like this can be useful in many ways, such as lending contrast or emphasizing the main color in a patterned fabric. It is one of the easiest ways to achieve a smart finish for an elegant overall look.

This simple border trim almost matches the curtain rod, framing each curtain for a simple contemporary feel.

A contrasting fringe helps the self-valance stand out against the curtain. Hung on a rod, this treatment offers the valance option while also maximizing the height of the window.

By incorporating the valance into the drapes, these curtains offer a cozy feel, but without restricting the light.

Large designs usually need extra yardage for the patterns to match. The rail-to-floor measurement may not finish at a complete pattern repeat vertically, so allow for one pattern repeat of wastage for each fabric drop. If you're joining widths, you'll also need to ensure that the pattern matches horizontally at the seams.

Strong patterns like this make enough of a statement in their own right and are in no need of extra trimming.

A shaped buckram valance, trimmed with tassels, brings the main interest to this window treatment. Here, it is set off by classic pencil-pleated drapes on a rail concealed behind the valance.

Full, generously gathered, floor-sweeping drapes, an elegant valance, and tiebacks create a sense of traditional style.

These curtains have not been gathered with heading tape. They have simply been made to double the length of the rod and rings have been hooked at regular intervals to the top of each drape. When slotted onto the rod, they fall into generous folds.

The heading may be traditional, but the bold horizontal stripes bring this treatment firmly into modern times.

Bottom-edge fringing is an excellent way to add a glamorous touch that is not too frilly. Silken fringes in muted tones, such as these, lend an early twentieth-century, Moulin Rouge feel. Brighter colors and firmer fibers give fringes a more updated, flirty feel.

The vibrant print and fringed hems have Arts and Crafts styling, while the wooden rod updates the look.

MODERN HEADINGS

Curtains have taken on a very different personality in recent years. The never-scrimp-on-fabric rule has taken a U-turn and now the reverse is true for an ultra-modern look. If minimal is your style, gathers are the new no-no. Think panels rather than drapes, as the idea is to enhance rather than shroud the window and, in turn, to complement the architecture of the room.

The cozy look is giving way to a feel that is more light and airy. This new move has been made possible partly because, with modern central heating and double glazing, we no longer need heavy drapes to keep out the cold in northern climates. It is also due to the daily influences of commercial buildings on our lives, such as shopping malls and offices, many of which are designed to be bathed in natural light. For this more pared-down look, heading tapes, rails, and elaborate hooking systems have been replaced by ties and curtain clips on rods or tension wires. You can either buy fabric as ready-made panels, or custom-make them by cutting fabric to fit the window and hemming all around. If you've time, stitch on tabs or ties; if not, simply clip them up with curtain clips and hang them on rods.

▶ Borrowed style

Metal shower-curtain hooks provide the perfect solution for window curtains as well. The large hooks provide a pleasing proportion to large windows.

▲ Feminine touch

Curtains cut slightly longer than the rod give depth and movement to the fabric without your having to add heavy gathers to the top. The flamboyant bow ties at the top make for a delightfully feminine modern heading.

▲ Romantic solution

Delicate ties on a white rod lend a feminine touch to an attic room. Although the heading is in the modern style, it perfectly complements the traditional Swedish-style furnishings, creating a refreshing update.

Shower-curtain hooks have been used for the drapes. As hooks are on show in modern window treatments, don't be shy of choosing large ones to make a statement.

The white-on-white scheme makes for a light look, despite several layers of draping.

MODERN HEADINGS: your choice

Although pared back compared to their traditional cousins, modern headings nevertheless play an equally important role in the whole look of a drape. Choose rivets or shackles for an architectural style, practical tabs for fuss-free interiors, or pretty ribbon ties for a feminine feel.

Many modern drapes are little more than a panel that is tied or held in place by tabs, clipped into position by curtain clips, or hooked by a number of means—all of which are designed to be shown off. There is a wide choice of custom-made hooks available, but you can find many others in unlikely places. Yachting retailers, for example, sell a huge variety of shackles, and a search in hardware and camping shops will reveal a variety of rings and hooks for original and attractive finishes. An easy solution for these "found" hooks and rings is to slot them into large, outsized eyelets, available from sewing shops.

Ribbon ties

Ultra-feminine ribbon ties make for easy modern headings. Just cut to length and stitch in place. These have been tied to a rod; they'd work just as well tied to curtain rings.

Big ties

Long curtains look better with more generous headings, and these chunky ties offer the perfect solution. They're contrast-lined to make more of a feature of the heading.

Button tabs

Enliven tab tops with button trims. Here, shell buttons add a feminine touch to delicate organza. Use chunky wood or covered buttons to vary the style.

Curtain clips

Use these simple and instant headings for clipping up ready-hemmed panels. There's a wide choice, ranging from this intricate scallop to simple metal crocodile clips.

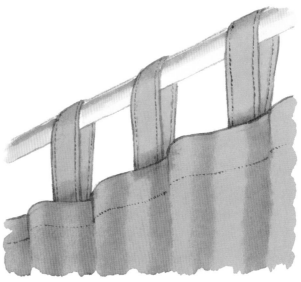

Tab tops

Fuss-free tab tops come stitched to many ready-made curtain panels. Buy the panels slightly wider than the window, then thread onto the curtain rod.

Rivet tabs

A variation on the button theme, riveted metal buttons bring a fashion feel to interiors. Jeans button kits are available from well-known sewing shops.

Shackles

For imaginative headings, look further afield than the local sewing shop. These shackles from yacht retailers, for example, make robust curtain fixings indoors or out.

RODS & FINIALS

Individual window style is expressed in the detail, and is greatly influenced by rod choice. Do you want to make a statement with your choice of rod, or would you prefer to be more understated? Wood is still very popular but metal now offers a wider choice—both in style and in finish—ranging from stainless steel and wrought iron to brass, nickel, and aluminum.

Rods are usually sold in kits, complete with rings and brackets, and they can be cut to size. Some metal rod kits come with notched sections that can be bent into shape around bay windows. Double-rail packs make a neat solution for window treatments, requiring both sheers and main curtains. It is sensible to choose your fabric first and then check the weight-bearing capability of each rod before buying.

▼ **Pretty holdups**
Wooden rods are a traditional way to hold up curtains, but they can take on a light and pretty contemporary feel when painted white with matching rings.

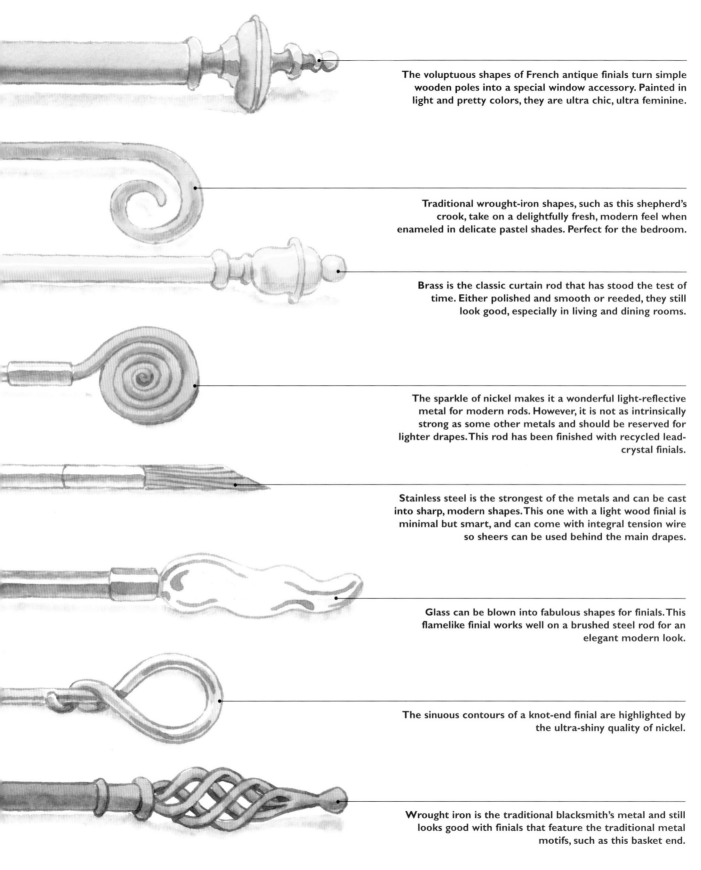

The voluptuous shapes of French antique finials turn simple wooden poles into a special window accessory. Painted in light and pretty colors, they are ultra chic, ultra feminine.

Traditional wrought-iron shapes, such as this shepherd's crook, take on a delightfully fresh, modern feel when enameled in delicate pastel shades. Perfect for the bedroom.

Brass is the classic curtain rod that has stood the test of time. Either polished and smooth or reeded, they still look good, especially in living and dining rooms.

The sparkle of nickel makes it a wonderful light-reflective metal for modern rods. However, it is not as intrinsically strong as some other metals and should be reserved for lighter drapes. This rod has been finished with recycled lead-crystal finials.

Stainless steel is the strongest of the metals and can be cast into sharp, modern shapes. This one with a light wood finial is minimal but smart, and can come with integral tension wire so sheers can be used behind the main drapes.

Glass can be blown into fabulous shapes for finials. This flamelike finial works well on a brushed steel rod for an elegant modern look.

The sinuous contours of a knot-end finial are highlighted by the ultra-shiny quality of nickel.

Wrought iron is the traditional blacksmith's metal and still looks good with finials that feature the traditional metal motifs, such as this basket end.

RINGS, CLIPS, & WIRES

The main function of curtain rings and clips is to provide a mechanism for hanging the drapes. But if they're going to be exposed, they may as well be beautiful! Before buying either, check their weight-bearing capability in conjunction with the rod or wire they are to be hung on. Heavy interlined drapes will need to be hung on robust rods with chunky rings, while sheers can be hung on almost anything, including tension wires threaded through rivets. Most wooden rings incorporate an eyelet designed to take a hook that can be fastened to the heading tape; fine metal rings can be sewn directly to the tops of lighter drapes.

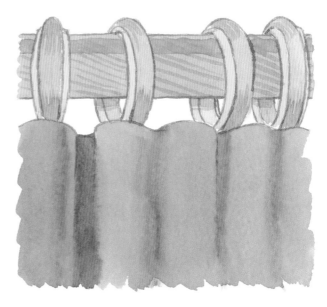

▼ Hooks on show

Undeniably, modern drapes look stunning hung on fine metal rods from oversized hooks that can be seen from a distance. The key is in the proportion—the longer the drapes, the larger the hooks can be.

Wooden rings

These antique, French-painted wooden curtain rings have moldings for added interest. Most modern equivalents are plainer and come in wood tones, black, cream, or white.

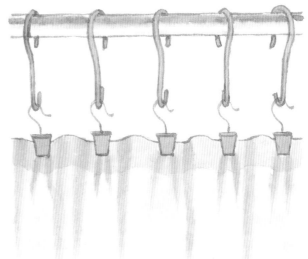

Clips with wire hooks

This attractive clip-and-hook combination enables curtains to be hooked onto rods or tension wires. They're only really suitable for sheers and light fabrics.

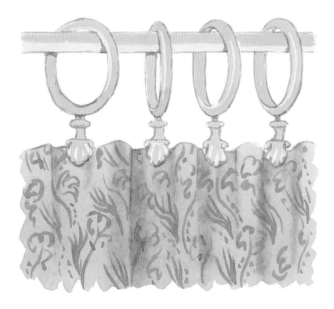

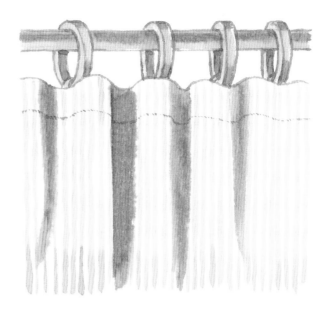

Shell wire clips

Pretty brass curtain clips with scallop detailing are inspired by antique equivalents, making them a good choice for use with both traditional and modern fabric designs.

Metal rings

Stainless steel rings on fine rods make a smart modern choice. The metal's strength means a rod can carry more weight than one of a similar diameter in a different material.

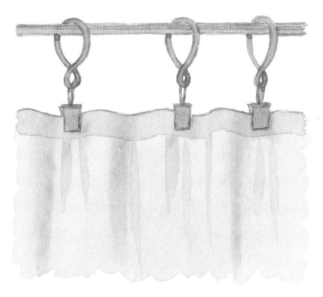

Eyelets on extension wires

Smart and simple, eyelets from sewing departments can be hammered through finished curtain tops, then threaded onto tension wires or fine rods.

Clips with rings

The large metal rings holding these curtain clips mean they can be used on larger-gauge metal rods. However, the clips will not be able to hold heavier drapes.

TOPS & TAILS

CURTAIN LENGTH

Drapes made in the same fabric, with the same heading and the same hanging gear, can still add a very different feel to a room, depending on their length. Full-length curtains always look elegant, even if the windowsill is some way off the floor, lending a sense of height to the ceilings. Sill-length curtains generally present a less formal feel, and these are often used in children's rooms or relaxed family rooms. They also have the advantage in that they don't cover up under-window radiators, thereby making for more efficient central heating.

As well as having a shortened hemline, curtains can also be shortened from the top. Café curtains are the traditional example of this, and although these are now less popular, they do have a very useful function. In ground-floor rooms where you want plenty of daylight but don't want to be seen by passersby, café curtains provide the perfect solution.

The windowsill length adds to the informal feel of these simple sheer curtains that run around three sides of the room.

▶ **Light plus privacy**
Plenty of natural daylight is a priority in rooms such as sunrooms, which are used predominantly during the day, yet there is a need for a feeling of privacy and a furnished look. These lightweight sheers, hung café-style at the windows on bamboo rods, are an ideal solution, contributing to a relaxed ambience without cutting out very much of the daylight.

▼ Full-length elegance

The longer the curtains, the more elegant the room looks. They don't even need to take into consideration the window—you can add length by installing the rod or valance at ceiling height, and by letting the curtains fall full length to the floor, even if the window is much smaller.

Letting the curtains fall into a puddle of fabric on the floor adds to the feeling of no-expense-spared opulence.

TRIMS &
TIEBACKS

tassels

fringes

bobbles

bows

beads

buttons

sequins

ribbons

braids

bullion

TRIMS & FRINGES

It's in the trims and fringes that the fun is to be had with window décor. These are the fashion touches; they are the elements that come and go, reflecting current trends. Some styles shun embellishment, such as wartime utility or sixties psychedelic, but most make use of trims.

There are trims that add a lush quality, such as deep fringing or tassel braids; there are others that bring a sense of fun, like bobbles, tufts, or brightly colored fringes. Some trims, such as piping, frills, and scallops, can even be made of curtain fabric to bring an element of movement, or as smart contrast for emphasis.

▲ **Rich fringe**
Dense antique fringing stitched to luxuriously lined and interlined drapes speaks of a past era when quality transcended cost.

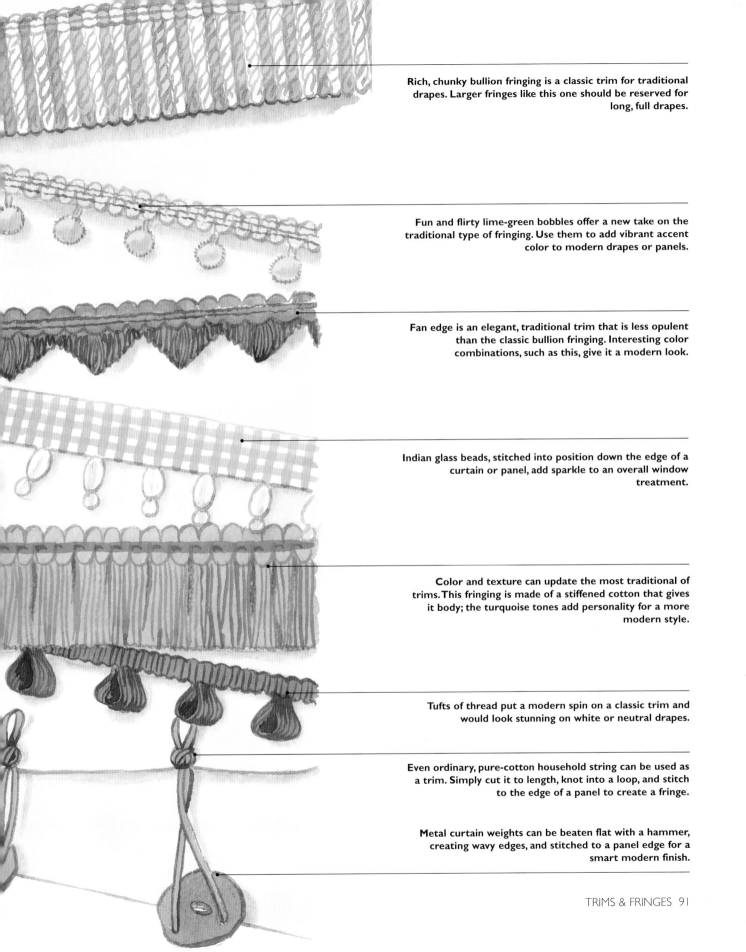

Rich, chunky bullion fringing is a classic trim for traditional drapes. Larger fringes like this one should be reserved for long, full drapes.

Fun and flirty lime-green bobbles offer a new take on the traditional type of fringing. Use them to add vibrant accent color to modern drapes or panels.

Fan edge is an elegant, traditional trim that is less opulent than the classic bullion fringing. Interesting color combinations, such as this, give it a modern look.

Indian glass beads, stitched into position down the edge of a curtain or panel, add sparkle to an overall window treatment.

Color and texture can update the most traditional of trims. This fringing is made of a stiffened cotton that gives it body; the turquoise tones add personality for a more modern style.

Tufts of thread put a modern spin on a classic trim and would look stunning on white or neutral drapes.

Even ordinary, pure-cotton household string can be used as a trim. Simply cut it to length, knot into a loop, and stitch to the edge of a panel to create a fringe.

Metal curtain weights can be beaten flat with a hammer, creating wavy edges, and stitched to a panel edge for a smart modern finish.

TASSELS

Whether they're full or fine, tassels make magnificently versatile curtain trims. Sewing stores stock a wide range, both in single tassels and in those that come in a strip woven to the edge of a braid. Contrasting colors make strong statements; bright primaries lend an extroverted feel. And for something more elegant, choose tassels that harmonize with the main fabric. Use tassel trims down the sides of curtains, along the bottom edge of valances, or stitched to the hems of panels.

▲ Traditional magnificence
Large silken tassels with elaborate weaving around the top section (the mold) are still often made by hand. Used as tiebacks, they bring lasting style to traditional drapes.

Tassel ties
The classic tassel takes on a wholly different look when made of natural jute. These chunky examples would be perfect for a relaxed modern look.

▶ Valance trim
A neat cream tassel lends emphasis to each point of a zigzag valance, bringing smart modern style to simple pencil-pleated curtains.

Even small tassels can make a design statement. Here they are stitched to the zigzag edge, emphasizing the valance, which is the main design element of the treatment.

Contrast tassels stand out. Being small, they would have been lost if they had been toned with the drapes. Instead, here they add accent.

TIEBACKS

Both practical and decorative, tiebacks offer plenty of scope for bringing individual style to window treatments. Tying back a curtain immediately lends it a different personality, bringing an extra dimension to the drape of the fabric. The tieback also acts as an accessory in the same way as does a fashion scarf or piece of jewelry. Classically, they're made from fabric that matches, coordinates, or even contrasts with the main curtain fabric, and they take on an almost upholstered feel. Modern interpretations bring endless choices, from simple ribbons, cords, or braids to heavy jutes, sometimes decorated with beads, sequins, shells, or buttons.

Jute tassel tieback
Natural jute, with its firm fibers, makes an eye-catching tassel. A single jute tassel, used as a tieback, gives a contemporary feel to a traditional treatment.

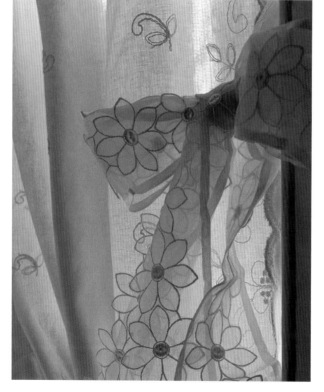

▲ Sheer delight
Diaphanous curtains are tied back in a bow using a strip of the same fabric. The appliquéd flowers give depth to the overall look.

Knot tieback
A variation on the bow tieback (opposite, above right), the knot has a softer feel than a simple fabric tieback, but it is not as overtly feminine as the bow.

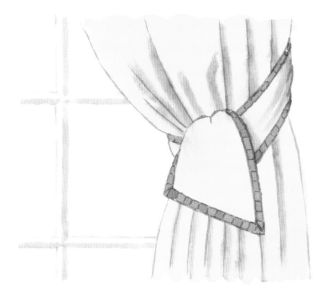

Contrast-trim tieback

Fabric tiebacks at their simplest are just lined and interlined strips of fabric. This one has a neat contrasting trim, smartening up the informal look.

Bow tieback

This tieback is made from two long sashes tied into a bow. With a ring at each end, which attaches to a hook behind the drape, the tieback can be unhooked when not needed.

Buckram tieback

Formal tiebacks are often cut to shape in a scallop and then finished with binding. This style is best used with long, full curtains.

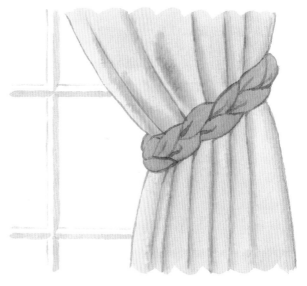

Braided tieback

Here's a simple but striking solution. Simply sew three tubes of fabric, braid them, and bind at the ends to create an interesting accessory for simple curtains.

HOLDBACKS

Pulled-back drapes can also be held in place by hold-backs. These are a more architectural option than tiebacks (see pages 94–95) and if this is your style, choose them when you buy the curtain rods as they are often sold in coordinated sets.

Usually made of wood or metal, holdbacks are smart and easy to use, as the drapes are simply pulled back and tucked in place. Beautiful holdbacks make a strik-ing accessory for dress curtains that are kept open. Experiment with their positioning before installing, bearing in mind that drapes generally look better with the holdbacks set higher, rather than lower.

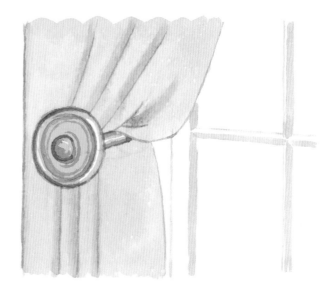

▼ Jewel style
This exquisite antique pressed-glass holdback adds a jewel-like quality to the drapes. If you are unable to find something similar, use an old glass cupboard knob.

Antique-painted wood
This beautiful antique French holdback, which has been made from painted hand-turned wood, is like a piece of sculpture in itself.

Aluminum with wood
Simple and modern, this holdback adds a touch of fun to the drapes. Paint the wooden finial to coordinate with the rest of the interior.

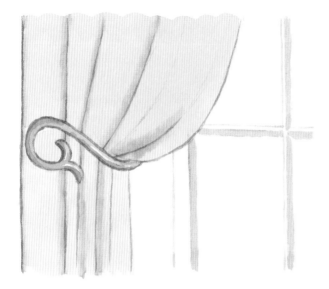

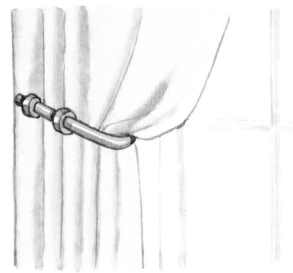

Enameled

Pretty pastel colors are possible with both enamel and powder-coated metal. The metal base material offers a wide choice of fluid shapes.

Stainless steel

This shiny material brings architectural style to modern interiors. Its strength enables stainless steel rods to hold a greater weight of fabric for their gauge than other metals.

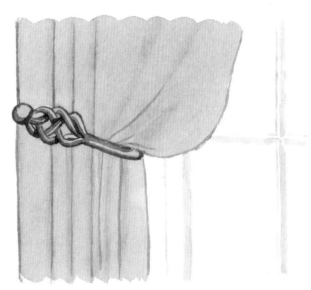

Antique brass

There are holdbacks in many delicate leaf and flower shapes, which work well in antique brass. They make an attractive option if you are planning to use holdbacks.

Wrought iron

The traditional blacksmith's material and craft have become hugely popular in recent years, adding timeless style to both traditional and modern window treatments.

VALANCES & PELMETS

swags

tails

smart

scarves

gathers

cornice boxes

elegant

lambrequins

box pleats

pretty

VALANCES, SWAGS, & SCARVES

Valances offer enormous scope for creative window treatments. They are useful tools for visually correcting windows that are mismatched, too high, too low, too small, or too large. Position valances high over low windows; make them wide over narrow windows; and cut them long for tall windows, or short for smaller windows. They look best when they are no deeper than one-fifth of the full curtain length; and shorter ones look best if they're not gathered, in which case add interest with box pleats or dogtooth edging.

Swags and tails are the ultimate in elegant top treatments. Best used on tall windows, they are made in two parts—the top swags, which could be single, double, triple, or even quadruple, and elegantly fashioned tails that frame the window.

▶ Double take
Simple buckram valances on top of draped scarves provide a dressed feel without shrouding beautiful window architecture. The choice of checked fabric and smart black trimming keeps the treatment city-smart, avoiding a tendency to be overly frilly.

▲ Subtle solution
Sometimes, just a hint of a valance is all you need to soften the window treatment. Here, a delicate garland is strung loosely across the top of the window, bringing individual style to the simple, semitranslucent curtain that hangs behind it.

▲ Dramatic draping
Densely woven silk in opulent gold, dramatically fringed in black, falls sensuously around a tall window. It is the perfect example of swags and tails that are elegant without being fussy. The swags and tails remain like this at all times while the white drapes are drawn and pulled back as needed.

The treatment works here because the room has high ceilings and tall windows.

The valance and scarf combination adds to the sense of grandeur.

VALANCES, SWAGS, & SCARVES: your choice

When choosing valance styles, study the proportions of both the room and the windows. Elaborate styles look best on taller windows in larger rooms, while simpler styles look good in smaller rooms, which can be in danger of being overpowered by ambitious window treatments. Add individual touches using trims, tassels, or fringes. When you are choosing a valance, remember that it will become the main feature of the treatment and will hide the heading of the drape, which is suspended behind the valance. So don't be tempted to use elaborate headings for the drapes; the best solution is to team interesting valances with simple pencil pleats.

Unstructured valance
Softly gathered and caught up under rosettes, this valance has a feminine feel that suits tall windows. Use a contrasting frill and rosettes to emphasize the look.

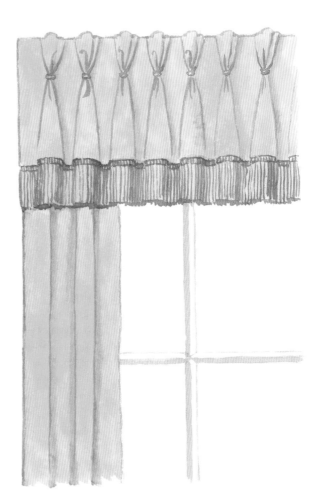

French-pleated valance
Any regular curtain heading can also be used for a valance. Here, smart French pleats trimmed with covered buttons and contrast fringing hang over pencil-pleated drapes.

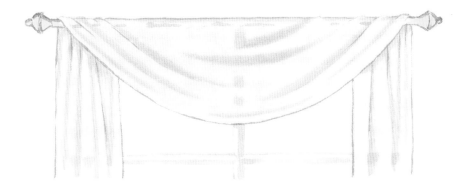

Simple scarf

This informal, no-sew scarf looks good in any style of interior— traditional or modern. It consists of a long piece of sheer fabric simply draped over an exquisite curtain rod, forming a panel that remains in front of the window.

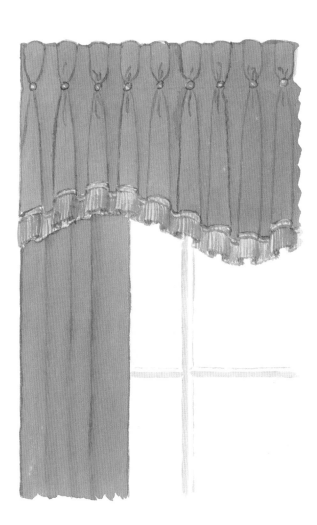

Serpent valance

As well as having a straight bottom edge, valances can be made with curved hemlines. They can be given Gothic arches or serpentlike curves, such as this one.

Three swags and tails

Wider windows can take more swags. This triple swag offers a smart solution for large windows in a well-proportioned room.

PELMETS & CORNICE BOXES

More architectural than their fabric cousins, pelmets (also known as fixed valances or lambrequins) are usually made of wood or chipboard. Designed to hide window treatment mechanics, at its simplest a pelmet can be a strip of wood covering the top of a window; or it can extend down the sides. At their most cunning, pelmets come disguised as part of the architecture itself—possibly as a matching cornice, set forward to allow space for the rail.

More commonly, however, pelmets are boxlike structures at the top of the window, ranging from utility basic to those that are prettily molded and painted. They can also be made from buckram, which is cut to shape, bent into a curve, and then covered with fabric. Once completed, the buckram pelmet is attached to a wood frame.

▶ French styling

Here, an elegant pelmet has been designed to team with the collection of eighteenth-century French antiques that furnish the room. Attention to detail—the hand-painted motifs and coach line painted along the shaped bottom edge—reinforce the style.

◀▼ Mirror fretwork

The scope of elegant creativity with pelmets is almost without limit. Here, a strip of wood over the window has been decorated with a delightful fretwork mirror frieze.

▼ Cream topping

This self-covered, hard buckram pelmet is cut and bent to the most beautiful of shapes. The curves are emphasized by tiny cream tassels.

The pelmet has enough restrained detail to set off beautiful cream drapes, embellished only with a subtle cream braid at the leading edge.

Curved detailing at the sides and center of the wide pelmet introduces interest along the whole width of the window without overwhelming the overall treatment.

PELMETS & CORNICE BOXES: your choice

Pelmets offer great versatility when it comes to window treatments. They can either be used as a feature to set off the drapes, or be disguised as part of the architecture. To make more of a feature of the pelmet, you could cut the bottom edge into elegant sweeping curves or geometric patterns (see below and opposite). Alternatively, install a simple boxlike shape and then add decoration with paint, molding, mosaic mirror, or any other cladding.

Buckram pelmets can be covered with fabric to match the drapes, then trimmed with braid, fringes, or tassels. Or search out interesting architectural detailing, such as a cornice, molding, or architrave, that can be used as a cornice box.

Shaped pelmets

Lend interest to the bottom edge of pelmets with curves or geometric designs. Use hard buckram and cut to shape with scissors; or with plywood, cut with a jigsaw and paint.

Lambrequins

Lambrequins cover the sides as well as the top of a window. This works especially well if the window is in a recess so the sides appear to be an extension of the wall.

Serpent curve

A pretty serpent curve makes for an elegant, classic pelmet that would work well with traditional drapes.

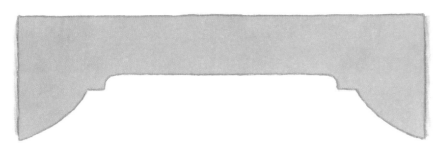

Edwardian mood

During the Edwardian era in the early twentieth century, the feminine curves of the Victorian look straightened out into a cleaner, more masculine style.

Medieval

Crisp "castellations" have a medieval fair look that can be fun in children's bedrooms, especially if the pelmet is brightly painted.

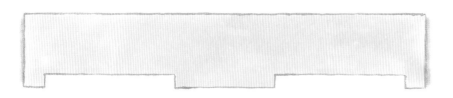

Smart geometric

Simple, subtle lines, such as these, are smart and modern, especially if the pelmet is cut sleekly slim.

Regency elegance

Romanesque lines were a popular feature of the Empire style of the early nineteenth century, providing an elegant finish for long drapes.

PELMETS: style options

Even given the same shape of pelmet, you can create completely different looks, depending on the choice of fabric and the way it is trimmed. For each of the pictures on these pages, a buckram pelmet was cut to one-fifth of the length of the drapes, and then given a simple curve for interest. Finally, the pelmet was covered with six different green fabrics and teamed with matching pencil-pleat curtains to demonstrate the effects of design and trimming.

DETAILS THAT COUNT

◆ **Proportion is a priority**—keep the depth of the pelmet to no more than one-fifth of the length of the curtains. Generally, pelmets look better on taller rather than wider windows.

◆ **A contrast trim** adds emphasis to the pelmet. Use either a restrained braid or piping, or go for a more flamboyant option with fringes, tassels, or sparkling beads.

◆ **The shape of** the bottom edge of a pelmet gives it character. Neat curves, such as the one featured on the examples on these pages, give a restrained feel; generous curves are more voluptuous, while scallops, dogtooth edging, or castellations add a sense of fun.

◆ **The pelmet itself** can be in a contrasting fabric to the drapes. This lends it more importance and looks best on tall windows teamed with slim pelmets.

◆ **Pelmets look best** over full drapes with a simple heading such as pencil pleats. Don't scrimp on fabric; aim to use double the width of the window.

White-striped edges smarten up this braid and, when stitched to the pelmet, create a neat chevron at the central point, which is echoed at the sides. Matching braid just inside the edges of the drapes coordinates the whole window treatment.

A wonderful allover leafy fabric design has been given emphasis by a smart braid in a tone that perfectly matches the print.

The woven braid, trimmed with tufted wooden beads, has a fun, modern feel. The fully beaded braid was used to trim the sides of the drapes, but when it came to the pelmet, every other one was snipped off to keep the look less cluttered.

Leaf-green fabric with fine horizontal stripes give the pelmet a slimmed-down look and lends the treatment an easy, relaxed feel.

The trim of cotton braid, plus wooden toggles, makes a witty statement that is bold enough to be seen from every corner of the room. The drapes were made to 1½ times the width so the fabric design was not hidden in too many folds.

A large fabric design needs extroverted treatment to set it off and a bold trim to make a loud enough statement.

Inspired by Native American textile design, this ikat stripe is set off by a raffia trim, softening the edges of the pelmet, and echoing the edges of the stripes.

The ikat-striped fabric is shown at its best here as it is laid flat on the generous pelmet.

The fresh nature of gingham is best left plain and simple, so no new trims have been introduced. Instead, the edges have been neatened with the same fabric cut on the bias and then used as a piping for the pelmet and bolder, broader binding for the drapes.

Green gingham gives this window a country style, while the tailored pelmet lends a smart, contemporary feel.

Fine cording stitched to the top and bottom of the pelmet offers a crisp finish that perfectly sets off the curve-and-pointed cut of the lower edge. This fine outlining is all you need to emphasize the pelmet when using subtle fabrics, such as this one.

A simple fabric design, set off by understated cream cording, makes for a classic window treatment.

SHADES, PANELS, & SHUTTERS

roman

pleats

wooden slats

split-cane

venetian

pinoleum

bamboo

austrian

london

roller

STRUCTURED SHADES

Smart and architectural, with a range of options for light control, structured shades generally give a crisp, contemporary feel to both period and modern houses. Installed within window reveals, they complement, rather than cover up, the architecture, with their sleek, light, and open look.

One of the main strengths of modern structural shades is the way each type is engineered to deal with light filtration. Some, such as Venetians and wooden-slatted shades, control the incoming light using fine louvers that can be adjusted to allow maximum light to enter or to block it out altogether. Others filter light through translucent or reflective fabric or paper. Some modern structural shades can even be made to pull up, rather than down, to allow full daylight in ground-floor rooms, while blocking out the prying gaze of passersby.

The pinnacle in pull-up shades are designed to fit the many different shapes of conservatory windows. Each shade is made to measure for the individual window, and this is the perfect solution for any other unusually shaped window in the house.

▶ **Outdoor style**
Split-cane, roll-up shades, with their natural look and unpretentious mechanism, are the perfect choice for a summerhouse. Their own weight ensures that they pull up and down smoothly using a yachting-inspired reefing system.

▲ **Pull-over**
Sleek, pleated conservatory shades are used here in a glass-roofed bathroom extension. Made to pull across the ceiling and down the windows, they protect the bather's privacy while complementing the architecture.

▲ **Wooden style**
Quieter to use and more solid than Venetians, wooden-slatted shades usually come in the natural wood colors. Here, the shades are supplied in a translucent milky finish for a light, modern look.

The natural tones of the cane are picked up in the colors of the paintwork and upholstery, creating an easy, relaxed look.

Cane roll-up shades are cut to fit, making them an ideal solution for awkward situations, such as corner windows.

STRUCTURED SHADES: your choice

The shades you choose depend partly on your style, partly on your need for privacy, and partly on how you want to deal with the light. Adjustable shades, such as Venetians and louvered-wooden slats (see below), are the perfect choice where you need control of both light and privacy. A smarter option than traditional nets, the louvers can be positioned to let in the light while simultaneously providing privacy. If there are certain times of the day when you need full, direct light, and you're not

worried about being seen, these shades can be simply pulled up. Vertical shades (see opposite) have a similar flexibility—they just open to one side instead of up.

When it comes to structural shades, size really does matter, as most have to be made to fit exactly within the architrave of each window. To ensure an exact fit of shade, ask a supplier to come and measure in your home. This makes for a neat finish and is especially valuable if you have any awkward-shaped windows.

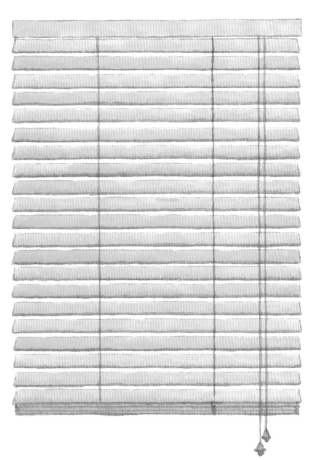

Venetian shade

Venetian shades are available in a wide range of colors with slats in various widths, and even perforated for a subtle, light-filtering quality.

Wooden-slatted shade

Elegance with a natural feel, these are the wooden cousins of Venetians. The louvers are usually heavier and larger, and they come in a range of woods and finishes.

Pleatex shade

These horizontally pleated shades in a heavy-duty paper or semitranslucent fabric are pulled up and down on fine cords and can fit awkwardly shaped windows.

Vertical shade

This businesslike option, often used in offices, brings a cool modern look to a room. The slats can be pivoted to any angle to shield the sun at all times of day.

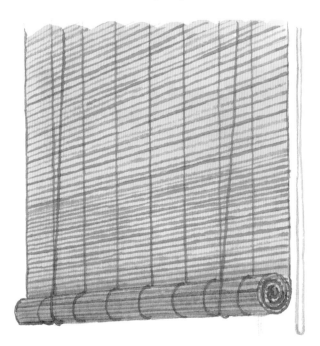

Pinoleum shade

Roll-up shades can be made from split cane, fine bamboo, or wooden strips interwoven with cotton thread. Some are fitted with a roller mechanism; others roll up.

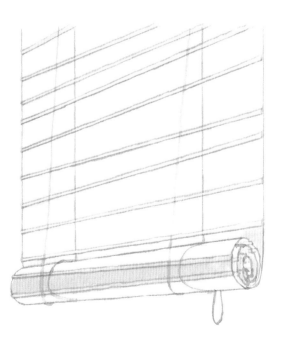

Paper shade

Translucent Japanese paper supported by bamboo strips makes a delightful and inexpensive light-filtering shade. These shades usually use a reefing mechanism.

SOFT SHADES

Soft shades successfully offer the sensual quality of drapes without masking beautiful window architecture, and, in that sense, they are a hybrid between rich traditional drapes and more minimal structural shades. With a choice that ranges from utility rollers to ultra-feminine Austrian, it is easy to custom make an individual look to suit any style.

Pretty shades, for example, offer an excellent solution when dealing with the perennial problem of getting around bay windows. Since most shades are made to measure, and each is attached directly onto the window frame, there are no rails or rods to bend around the corners. Smart but simple shades, such as rollers or Romans, can also be teamed with drapes as part of fuller window treatments. Shades are particularly useful where there are fixed drapes. Simply leave the drapes undisturbed and, as night approaches, pull the shades down to shut out the dark.

▶▲ Roman elegance

The most versatile shades of all, Romans can be used on their own, as here, or teamed with fixed drapes. Folding neatly onto themselves, they look smart up or down. This wonderful white antique linen is the perfect fabric to use as it is heavy, and the pulley system of Roman shades uses their weight as part of the mechanism.

▶ Candy stripes

Not all tie-up shades have to be simple—these pink-and-cream striped ones have a chic feminine feel that's enhanced by ties and rosettes.

▶▶ Shabby chic

A cross between an Austrian and a London, this shade in cream linen brings a soft, dressed look to the window. Pleated rather than gathered, it looks sharper than a gathered-top Austrian, while several drawstrings across the width make it more voluptuous than a London shade.

With fabric matching the walls of the room, the shade brings a subtle yet undeniably pretty feel to the room.

Heavy cream-colored linen enhances the generous, voluptuous folds in the shade.

SOFT SHADES: your choice

Whether they're smart, tailored Roman or elaborately gathered and frilled Austrians, less structured shades bring an element of drapery to the windows, yet use much less yardage than traditional drapes. It was the Swedish who introduced the widespread use of shades. Sweden was one of the first countries to utilize central heating and double glazing, and, freed from the need to use heavy drapes for heat conservation, developed a love of simple roll-up shades secured by ties or a reefing system. These unpretentious shades also have the advantage of allowing in maximum natural light—a precious commodity in the north, where winter daylight hours are so short.

The mechanisms of soft shades range from spring-loading rollers to pulley systems. If it is flexibility you are after, choose a pulley system or use pull-up cords rather than a spring-loaded roller.

Roller shade
Made from any stiffened fabric wound onto a sprung roller and attached to the top of the window, roller shades roll up neatly, allowing for maximum light.

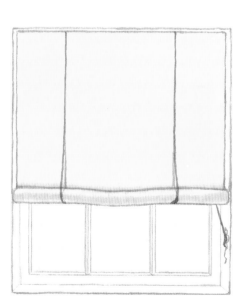

Swedish shade
These simple fabric shades roll up from the bottom on a reefing system. Economical on fabric, they bring a fresh and pretty look to any window.

Tied shade
A variation on Swedish shades, these are simply rolled up by hand and fastened into position using ties stitched to the top of the shades at the back and front.

Roman shade

Supporting battens slipped between lining and main fabric keep Roman shades looking tailored. If using a sheer fabric, use fine dress stays designed for corsetry instead of battens.

London shade

With no supporting battens, London shades are softer than Roman shades. If you're making them in sheer fabric, use ribbon, rather than cord, to pull them up.

Austrian shade with tails

Austrian shades are all pulled up on cords from the bottom to a gathered top. Here, tumbling tails are created by the outermost cords lying a little in from the edges.

Austrian shade with gathered frill

For a fuller effect, use tightly gathered pencil pleats at the top and add a frill all round. The three pull-up cords are positioned equally across the width.

ROMAN SHADES: style options

Used plain and simple on their own, or teamed with traditional drapes, Roman shades can enhance any interior. Set your own style with clever choices of fabrics and trims.

DETAILS THAT COUNT

◆ **Adjust fabric designs** that don't quite fit your window dimensions. Do this by taking two widths of fabric, cutting them appropriately, and then stitching them together.

◆ **Antique monograms** and bold motifs can be cut out and appliquéd to the front of a Roman shade for interest, whether it is pulled up or let down.

◆ **Ribbons make attractive** pull-cord substitutes. They are especially effective on sheer shades as they can be seen from the front through the translucent fabric.

◆ **Fabrics with borders** provide perfectly coordinated trims. Simply cut them off and reapply as edgings, hems, stripes, or trims.

◆ **Achieve an affordable** couture look by using luxurious trims on shades made from utility fabrics.

Although this paisley design is bold, the motif is small enough to allow plenty of flexibility when it comes to working out the fold sizes.

The glass bead trim adds elegance and weight to the bottom edge of this shade, making it easier to move up and down.

The vertical nature of this design means the fabric position has to be planned carefully. The vertical stripes have been centered on the window, and the shade cut a little wider to allow for the two half repeats at the edges.

Here, pretty drop-tail edges and elegant silk tassels along the bottom edge complement a flamboyant palm tree design.

Carefully plan the positioning of large motifs. Here, one "cameo" has been centered at the top of the shade so that the repeat is a diamond pattern.

Eye-catching motifs, such as these, are better used on large windows as the first fold needs to be fairly deep.

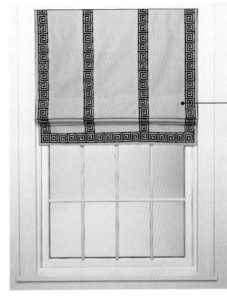

The braid runs both horizontally and vertically and the border is inset by ¼ in. To ensure the Greek keys are aligned along the bottom, the center panel is slightly wider than the sides.

A gold Roman shade looks smart when trimmed with an equally striking Greek key-design braid.

The coordinating red trims on this shade were originally the selvage borders. Since the window is narrower than the fabric width, the borders were cut off and repositioned to make a striking design.

The drop tails at the foot of this shade add a soft, feminine touch designed to complement the fabric pattern.

A template of the motif was enlarged to fit the shade and then appliquéd into position using a pearl stitch (a tight zigzag). If you want to try this, make sure the stronger background fabric does not show through. If it does, line the white first.

The bold motif has been cleverly designed to look good whether the shade is up or down.

PANELS

Panels are the new drapes. Gather-free, they can be hung by tab tops, ties, or clips, serving to dress the window without masking it, to filter light, and to preserve privacy. A whole new thinking on window treatment, a panel offers the softness of a curtain with the subtlety of a shade. If you love textiles, make the most of fabulous prints by hanging them flat. Alternatively, choose the most exquisite fabrics—you'll need a fraction of the yardage required for traditional drapes, so material that is better quality will be within your budget. Cut panels a little wider than the window to allow for gentle movement. You can also add interest with trimmings, such as beads, fringes, sequins, or even feathers.

▶ **Simply modern**

Sheer panels fitted within the floor-to-ceiling reveals of these tall windows let light flood into the room, lending a light and airy feel. Free from gathers, the translucent fabric allows the lines of the window frames to show through, retaining a sense of their architecture within the room.

▼ **Lacy detail**

If panels are generally too plain for your taste, indulge yourself in some feminine touches, such as lacy fabric or sheers with lacy borders. This panel has been threaded onto a café rod that is installed on the reveals, and the overall effect is one of romantic harmony.

Stiff cotton organdy in pure white is naturally light reflective. It is loosely woven and has plenty of body, even after it has been washed, making it the perfect fabric for sheer panels.

Panels can either be fitted within the reveals, as here, or hung on rods mounted above the window.

PANELS: your choice

The clean, simple lines of panels have made them a popular modern choice. Used flat and attached to the architrave, they are unfussy and enhance, rather than cover up, a window's architecture. In parts of Europe, lace panels traditionally were used for privacy, and teamed with heavier drapes that were pulled across the window for warmth. Modern heating and glass technology have dispensed with the need to provide coziness, so panels have moved from supporting roles to star players. Their appeal is their economy on fabric, so you can afford to splurge on glorious woven silks or finely embroidered organdy; choose to decorate them with sequins or beads, or add exquisite trims. Hang your panels by curtain clips, tabs, or ties, or feed onto rods.

Portière panel
Traditionally the method for hanging curtains at doors, portière rods can also be used for suspending panels at windows to create dreamy fabric "shutters."

Lace panel
Popular in continental Europe, lace panels make a delightful alternative to net curtains. Some panels come in wonderful designs featuring birds, flowers, and leaves.

This border has been made from a broad ribbon, mitered at the corners, and stitched into position.

Cut simple leaf motifs from contrasting fabric. The sheer panel allows the glazing bars to show through, and these can be used as part of the design with one motif positioned at the center of each windowpane.

Border lines

The cheapest sheer fabrics can be given weight and style with the addition of a smart braid or denser fabric border. This is also an excellent way to add color.

Appliqué panel

Flat panels make the perfect subject for appliqué. Cut shapes or embroidery from antique or printed fabrics, then appliqué them onto panels for a unique design.

SHADES, PANELS, & SHUTTERS

SHUTTERS & SCREENS

Traditionally, wooden shutters were part of the window architecture and most were designed to deal with the local climate. Georgian shutters folded neatly back on themselves within the window reveals, ready to be closed against the cold and dark winter nights of the north. In the sunny Caribbean, however, louvered plantation shutters had quite a different function. Usually kept closed, they shielded the interior from the dazzle and heat of the noonday sun, while allowing the light to filter through the louvers.

With central heating and air conditioning, we now have the luxury of choosing our shutters purely from a style perspective. A favorite with modern architects because they enhance rather than camouflage elegant lines, shutters and screens now come in many new materials, such as sandblasted glass, polypropylene, and metal mesh. They can be hinged in position or set on runners at the window for sliding screens.

Although shutters are designed to cut out the light or glare from the sun, those that are brightly painted create a sunny atmosphere.

▲ Half measures
Half-sized plantation shutters mean plenty of light can flood through at the top of the windows, while offering privacy at street level. This is the perfect solution for living rooms or workrooms.

▲ Bright spark
Shutters offer a smart solution in a room with two sets of French doors and a large window. Drapes would have made opening the doors less than easy and, with the number of curtains, overcrowded the room visually.

The shutters can be opened and closed in turn throughout the day to cut out the sun's rays as they move around the room.

▲ Screen saver

Screens are like moveable shutters and can be positioned wherever they are needed. This one is lower than the window so it allows light in at the top, while screening glare lower down.

▲ Plantation perfection

Plantation shutters with adjustable louvers offer a flexible window treatment that sets off the architecture. The louvers can be adjusted to cut out glare, and whole shutters can be opened to let in light when it's needed.

SHUTTERS & SCREENS: your choice

If, like most of us, shutters don't come as part of the architecture in your home, you have two options. Either have some made to measure and hinged in place, or position freestanding screens at the window. If you choose to use hinged screens, they can be left partly opened or closed in much the same way as traditional Georgian shutters, but even given this basic style you can create completely different looks, depending on what the panels are made of.

Wood is obviously the most traditional material for a shutter. For a smart contemporary feel, choose sand-blasted glass or pierced sheet metal. If you want something a little softer or prettier, look at painted fretwork. These various materials can also be incorporated into sliding panels for contemporary window screens.

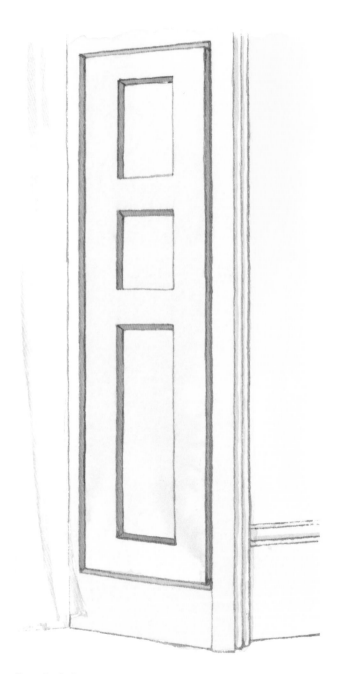

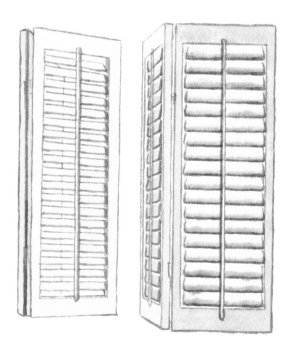

Plantation shutter

Shutters with adjustable louvers provide flexibility throughout the day. Often made in two halves, the top can be opened for extra light, while the bottom is closed for privacy.

Paneled shutter

This traditional-style shutter folds neatly into the window reveals. Many people nowadays keep these open and team them with a sheer panel for privacy.

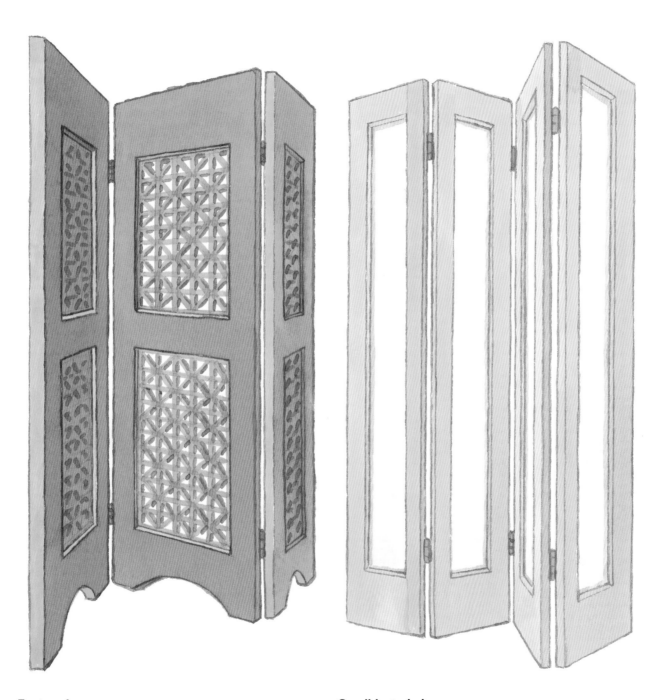

Fretwork screen

Freestanding screens can be used at windows, giving the appearance of shutters. These have been made using fretwork panels that are bought, cut to size, and painted.

Sandblasted glass screen

Set sandblasted glass screens at the window for soft, filtered light while securing privacy. To let in more natural light, have them made to three-quarters the height.

MEETING THE CHALLENGE

MAKING IT WORK

Planning beautiful window treatments is all very well in principle, but not all of us have perfectly proportioned rooms with windows ideally positioned to accommodate the drapes we adore. Alternatively, we may have awkward window shapes to deal with.

Unusually shaped windows are very often a feature of the room, so don't necessarily rush to cover them up unless you need the privacy. If you do need the privacy, it's important to come up with solutions that don't hide the greatest asset in the room. Shades that fit within the shape of the window can be an excellent solution, and if your style is modern, you have the option of choosing light, pretty, structured conservatory shades, which can be made to almost any shape in a wide choice of colors. Many can be made to pull up, rather than down, and so can accommodate unusually shaped tops. Such shades don't have to be restricted to sunrooms, and can look stunning in other rooms (see page 112 for a bathroom example).

▶ Top treatment
Install extra-long curtain rods well above round-topped windows so their elegant curves can be fully appreciated. Give them tie- or holdbacks, too, to ensure that the drapes remain well away from the window frame.

▼ French-door style
Drapes hanging over inward-opening French doors are awkward to use, so here, pretty curtain panels have been threaded onto a café rod that is attached directly to the doors.

However, windows that are far from attractive, or that sit unhappily in the room, very often need help. Their proportions can be visually adjusted using rods or valances fitted high or cut long; with clever use of color, or with fabrics that are fine or bulky. The ultimate shape-changing tool you have at your disposal is a lambrequin. This is a fixed valance that surrounds the whole of a window in a recess (see page 106). In the eighteenth century, lambrequins were used for elaborate window dressing, but, nowadays, they can be used to visually "clean-up" badly proportioned modern windows.

◀ ◀ **Pivoting problems**
Louvered shades installed directly onto pivoting windows both look extremely smart and do not interfere with opening and closing. Furthermore, they give complete control over light and shade.

▼ **Bay tradition**
Swags and tails dressing each window provide a delightful traditional treatment for this bay as it does not rely on a rod that would need to be bent into position.

◀ **Into the eaves**
Although these windows are regular in shape and proportion, the attic ceiling above them created an incongruous shape. The solution? A piece of fabric was cut to fit right up to the ceiling, and London shades were attached beneath.

MEETING THE CHALLENGE

TRANSFORMING THE UPRIGHT

Where window proportions are less than elegant, clever window dressing is the solution. Here, the principles of design should be similar to those applied when choosing an outfit: aim to disguise less flattering features, while accentuating the positive.

Pleasing architectural proportions make for a relaxed ambience. It is difficult to come up with quick fixes for walls in the wrong position, but there is a lot you can do for windows, in a way that can dramatically change the whole look of the room.

For windows that are tall and narrow, widen them by installing an extra-long curtain rod, so the curtains can be pulled beyond the architrave. This successfully gives the illusion of added width. If the reverse is your problem—tall windows that are also very wide—slim them down with drapes that have full gathers (see pages 74–75) and which are always kept partly drawn over the windowpanes.

Low and small windows can be transformed too. Lend height to low windows by raising the curtain rod or pelmet, or by incorporating the pelmet into the cornice. This works best if the walls and curtain fabric are similar colors. Open out close-set windows by treating them as a single unit with only one curtain on either side. Enlarge small windows by installing long curtain rods and high pelmets so the finished treatment hangs clear of the window area, letting as much light as possible into the room.

▶ **Two in one**
These beautiful Georgian-style windows have exquisite proportions, but, set so close, they could easily look pinched and narrow if individually dressed. Yet by using just one pair of drapes to cover both windows—one curtain at each end of the wall—the windows' width rather than height has been emphasized.

A fine metal rod spanning both windows visually transforms two narrow windows into one, immediately making them look more generous.

By using one, rather than two, curtains for each window, more light streams into the room.

A fine fabric does not create too much bulk, complementing the architecture and opening up the narrow windows.

▲ Gaining height

Although already tall, this window was in danger of being dwarfed by the four-poster. But by positioning the rod well above the window, the window appears taller, and the extra long drapes add elegance to the whole room.

▲ Slim-line solution

The proportions of this squat window have been completely transformed in two ways. The ceiling-height pelmet immediately makes the window look taller, while silken drapes disguise the sides, slimming it down. The overall effect changes the whole character of the room, making the ceiling appear loftier.

FRENCH DOORS

The main question with French doors is, Do you heavily drape them to protect against rapid heat loss through glass, or do you aim for a seamless boundary between indoors and out to bring in a sense of the outdoors? If you have (or can fit) modern double or triple glazing, the heat loss can be taken out of the equation, leaving you free to choose the most minimal panel, or even no window treatment at all, if that is your taste. Most French doors open outward, though some open inward and can become tangled with the window treatment. The solution is to use a long curtain rod so that the drapes can be pulled clear of the hinge when opening, or to install rods onto the door.

▶ Smart solution

The contrast between white paint and dark wood in the hall is the inspiration for the white curtains. Bound in black and hung on a single dark rail, the curtains link the spaces and visually open the entrance hall.

▼ Inward problem

Where French doors open inwardly, and there is no space for the curtains to be drawn back far enough to allow the doors to open, install curtains directly onto the door. These light sheers, gathered onto a curtain wire, provide privacy, yet open and shut as one with the door.

The off-white, floor-to-ceiling drapes match the walls, so almost disappear, while the dark borders imply an alternative, taller door.

Medium-weight fabric does not provide too much bulk at the window, yet helps to keep out the winter cold.

▲ Tall story

To let in maximum light, set the rod well above the top of the French doors and, if possible, make it long enough to allow the curtains to be drawn back clear of the glass.

▼ Perfect framing

Tall French doors leading onto balconies of Victorian houses are more for architectural interest than for constant use. These classic velvet drapes set them off exquisitely.

ARCHED WINDOWS

Beautiful arched windows were a feature of Queen Anne architecture of the early eighteenth century in England. It is a style that deserves to be shown off, rather than shrouded in yards of fabric, though there are times when the need for privacy or warmth means you need to compromise.

There are three main ways of using drapes to deal with arched windows. One is to set a long rod well above the window so that the curtains can be opened clear of the architrave and can show off the beautiful architecture. Another is to set the rod or wire below the curved top, along the horizontal glazing bar, and dress just the lower part of the window. The third solution is to attach the gathered top around the curved part of the window so that it frames the elegant lines rather than fighting with them.

▶ Taking shape

The classic architecture of full-length windows is shown off with diaphanous drapes that are shaped around the tops. The one that is used as a door has not been dressed, to allow for easy opening.

◀▼ High priority

The curtain rod is positioned high above the window to show off the elegant curved top. The cream curtains almost match the walls, visually receding, and so avoid dominating the pretty window.

▼ Alternative curves

Here, it is the archway into the window recess that is curved, rather than the windows themselves. The windows have been dressed in blue tartan to match the wallpaper, setting off the graceful lines of the cream-painted arches.

The translucent quality of sheer fabric allows for a full treatment, while showing off the graceful shape of the windows.

The sheers are pulled back to the point where the curve straightens out, so framing rather than shrouding the elegant lines of the window.

MEETING THE CHALLENGE

SMALL WINDOWS

Small windows aren't necessarily a problem in themselves, but sometimes their proportion in relation to the rest of the room can present challenges. If the windows look incongruous in any way, they can be corrected with curtain rods or valances used overly long or set high. You can also cut the curtains long—even to floor length—to give small windows more of a presence in the room.

If the windows are well-proportioned within the room, you need to use a very different ploy. Choose a neat solution, such as a Roman or roller shade that fits within the architrave so the window does not dominate the room. Choose a fabric in a subtle color, which will not detract from its surrounding. A prettier solution could be to gently swag a delicate length of lace over a fine wooden curtain rod, or to attach a simple sheer panel that would just "dress" the window without restricting the light.

▲ **Lace enlargement**

This tiny cottage window is visually expanded with the full lace treatment of curtains and valance that frame the window without infringing on the opening. The translucent quality of the fabric means that maximum light is let in and yet it contrasts interestingly with the window frame, painted dark green.

◀ **Streamlined solution**

This bathroom window is in perfect proportion to the room, which is shown off by a smart Roman shade that fits neatly within the architrave. The cream fabric adds subtle variety against the white woodwork.

▶ **Small but beautiful**

Three windows "punched" into the gable wall of this converted barn may be small, but they're carefully proportioned and positioned. The aim here is to show off, rather than interfere with, a clever architectural solution. The bamboo roller shades do just this.

The hard-to-reach top shade is left permanently down, looking good at all times of night and day.

Smart split-cane shades fit perfectly into the window reveals. Their color echoes that of the exposed wood beams.

BAY WINDOWS

Bays can be curved or square, and what these shapes have in common is the problem of getting the curtains to glide easily around the corners. Generally, curtain tracks can be bent, and then concealed with valances. Metal rods, too, can be bent, but this is a little more tricky. You either need to find some that are made with sections that have been cut so that they can be bent, or you have to have them specially made. This can involve complicated cross-measuring to ensure that the angles are right, but once it has been done, the drapes will move gracefully around the bay. Another solution is to use shades that fit within the architraves of each window within the bay.

When Roman shades are fully pulled up, they almost disappear, showing off the pretty architecture of bay windows.

▲ Valance link

Roman shades provide a smart bay-window treatment, but here, the large mullions make strong, distracting divisions. The solution has been to add a valance that spans all the windows, bringing a horizontal link across the bay.

▶ Shades and sheers

The bay window of this town house looks onto the street and so is very exposed when the shades are raised. The solution is to fit neat, sheer café curtains.

Fitting within the architrave of each individual window, shades of any type—Roman, roller, London, or Austrian—automatically fit the shape of the bay.

Smart geometric fabrics, such as gingham, perfectly suit the tailored look of Roman shades.

CORNER WINDOWS

The main dilemma with corner windows is whether you want to accentuate the corner, or whether you prefer the look of full drapes, because when windows touch each other at a corner, the two are not compatible. If you choose the drape route, the two curtains will soften the corner where they meet. This can lend a soft but exotic tented look. For a more architectural look, the solution has to be similar to bays, with shades of all types being the easiest option. When these are rolled or pulled up, the room takes on a wonderfully outdoorsy feel, with light pouring in from two areas.

▲ Light fantastic

Informal, cream roll-up Swedish shades, dressing a generous corner window, make for a bright, light-flooded country house feel. As the sun moves around the room, the shades can be individually raised and lowered. The setting is perfect for informal lunches.

These custom-made louvered shutters were designed at the building stage of this light-flooded room to ensure that the corners fitted exactly.

The individually adjustable louvers mean they can be opened and closed successively during the day to cut out any glare as the sun moves around.

Natural-colored wood creates a pleasing and relaxing ambience.

◀ **Architectural control**

Louvered shutters provide an architectural solution to the problem posed by corner windows. They need to be specially designed so they do not clash at the hinges when they are being opened or closed.

MEETING THE CHALLENGE

MISMATCHED WINDOWS

Not all windows match or mirror each other in an ordered fashion that is pleasing to the eye, and sometimes you will find that visual adjustments need to be made. Two windows of different dimensions can be made to look the same size with the use of drapes and valances that cover the architraves. For example, a valance can be positioned low on a high window and high over a low window with both sets of curtains cut full length to give the illusion that both windows are the same size.

Sometimes, mismatched windows are an architectural feature that should be emphasized, rather than hidden. In this case, consider them together to ensure they complement each other.

▲ **Streamlined solution**
These windows match in height, but not in width, so the solution is to pull them together with a single color that has been used on the walls, pillar, and curtain fabric. While the large window has two curtains, the smaller one has only one, making the window seem wider.

Windows and doors of very different dimensions can make a room lack harmony, but in this one, a narrow window, two doors, and a wide window are fitted with neat, pleated shades, which help considerably to unify the room.

Even the doors are fitted with matching shades, which have been attached directly to the frames for easy opening and closing.

Although the windows are different sizes, they become a good architectural feature when lent cohesion by tailor-made blinds.

◀ Making the best of it

This wall is made up of a series of windows and doors of very different dimensions that could pose a design problem. Here it has been solved with pleated shades, individually cut to fit each window and door. The overall result is a smart solution that enhances rather than shrouds the architectural features of the windows.

WORKSHOP REFERENCE

MEASURING

Whether you want curtains or shades, accurate measuring is vital for a smart end result. It is best to use an extendable steel tape, as it does not stretch, and you will need to measure at least twice to double-check the dimensions, especially if installing shades, which need to fit the window more precisely than drapes.

The first step is to fit the rod, track, or wire for drapes, or the top batten for the shade. For drapes, the rod or track should extend at least six inches on either side of the window—more if desired. For shades, the batten is usually fitted to the front edge of the architrave at the top. However, if the window is recessed, drapes and shades can be fitted successfully either within the recess or to the outside edge. Before reaching that stage, however, you must measure your window both for finished width and for finished length.

1 Finished width

Accurately measure the full length of the rail, rod, or batten. If the drapes are hung from a rail with a return, then add this to the width.

2 Finished length

Establish how long the treatment should be: sill length, to the top of the radiator, or floor length. Next, measure from the top of the track, rod, or batten, or, if you're using a wooden rod with rings, then measure from the bottom of the rings to the sill or floor, depending on the length of the treatment. Traditional drapes usually hang ½ inch clear of the floor. If you want them to "puddle" onto the floor, add between one inch and four inches to the finished length.

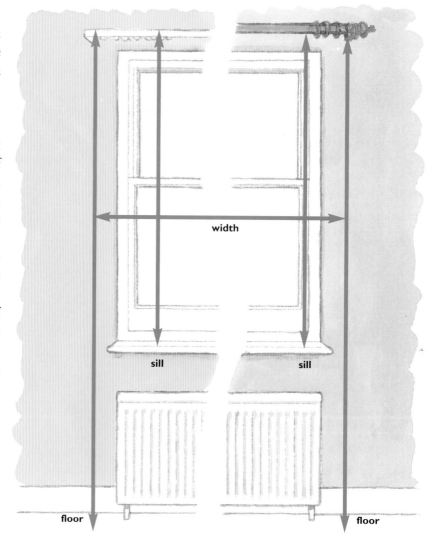

Measuring for curtains

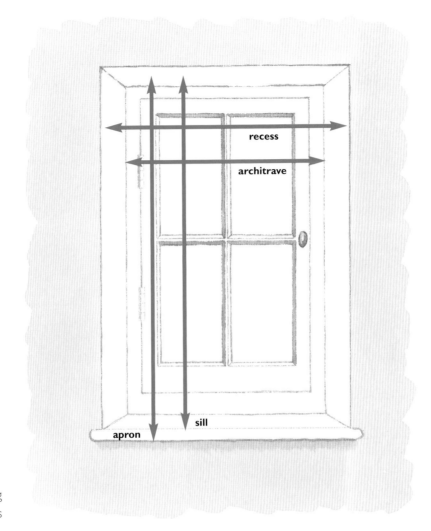

recess

architrave

sill

apron

Measuring
for shades

Estimating fabric for drapes

◆ Work out the length by adding eight inches to the finished length measurement for headings and hems.

◆ Next, choose a heading and select the tape. Each tape is marked with the fullness required—usually around 2 to 2½ times the length of the rod or rail (see also pages 74–75). This will give you the width of the ungathered drape.

◆ To work out how many drops you will require for each drape, divide this measurement by the width of the fabric.

◆ Multiply the number of drops by the curtain length to give you the required yardage.

Estimating fabric for shades

◆ Add five inches to the finished length for hems. For shades that are gathered vertically, you may want to add to the finished length to allow for ruching, even when the shade is down.

◆ If the shade is to be gathered at the top—as in an Austrian shade, for example—work out the number of drops in the same way as for curtains. If the shade is flat—for example, Roman—simply add four inches for side turnings to the finished width and then divide by the fabric width for the amount of drops.

◆ If the shade requires more one than drop, you should always add extra for seam allowances.

HIDDEN TRACKS & HOOKS

Hidden tracks are the unsung heroines of traditional window treatments. Nowadays, they're usually made of PVC, which can be bent around bays, and, when teamed with PVC hooks or fittings, the result is a smooth, gliding action for the drapes. There are also tracks designed to be used on their own for simple curtains, and others that work in teams to allow for valances and other multilayered effects. Choose the basic versions for a manual pull or corded for an automatic draw.

Most tracks come with gliders that have small rings to take the hooks on the heading tape. Other tracks also have integral hooks to slide into the heading tape. Choose one to suit your requirements.

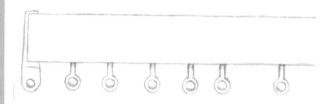

Basic PVC curtain track
Most basic PVC curtain tracks can be bent into bays. Most are fitted with small ring gliders to accommodate curtain hooks.

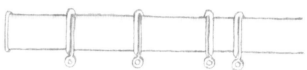

Hooked track
This track has gliders that incorporate hooks and rings to neatly accommodate main drapes and sheers within one rail. These are particularly useful for "dress" curtains that are not designed to be drawn together.

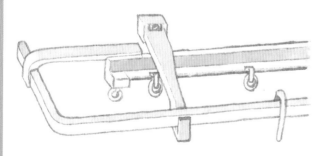

Double track
These are designed for curtains and valances. Different sets are designed to hold different weights of curtain, so take a fabric sample plus window measurements to the store and ask for advice on the correct type for your treatment.

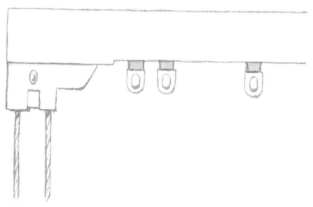

Corded track
For smooth, silent opening and closing, with just one pull on a cord, choose a corded track.

Net track

This extendable track can be threaded through the tops of simple nets and lightweight curtains, automatically gathering up into a heading.

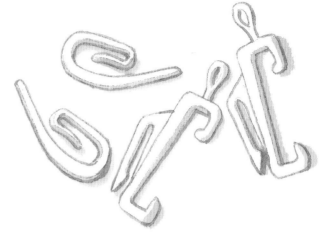

Net wire

This delightfully simple option of plastic-coated wire, fastened in place with screw hooks and eyes, is still a popular option.

Ready-made tape hooks

There are various basic hooks available for use with ready-made tapes that have special pockets to accommodate them. Here are three examples: one is attached directly to the rail; the other two slide into the pockets, then hook onto the rings on the rail.

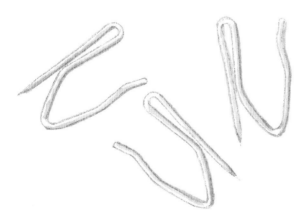

Hooks for handmade headings

The sharp points of these hooks are used to pierce through hand-sewn buckram headings. The other end hooks through the rings.

Specialized hooks

The more elaborate headings, such as pinch pleat and goblet, also offer the option of specialized hooks. These two, which can be used with pinch pleats of different sizes, give a neater finish than standard hooks.

TAPES, CORDS, & OTHER NOTIONS

The key to creative window treatments lies in the headings. Traditionally, these were pleated or gathered by hand, requiring careful measurement and meticulous checking. But life has been made a lot easier with ready-made heading tape containing fine cords that can be gathered up to create quickly and easily perfect pleats or gathers. They also incorporate special pockets for curtain hooks; others incorporate rings or pockets for the vertical cords used to pull up Roman, Austrian, and London shades. Choose your preferred heading from pages 74–75 and then find the tape to suit.

In addition to the items illustrated on these pages, other notions that are useful for window treatments include wooden acorns to tidy the gathered pull-up cords for shades, and cleats for winding the cords around to keep the shades in the "up" position.

Standard tape
The basic ½-inch ready-made tape with pockets and gather cords. This type of tape is perfect for lightweight curtains and sheers.

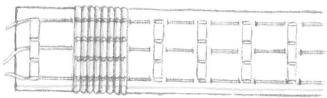

Pencil pleats
This tape creates neat, regular gathers. The heading tape for pencil pleats is available in two-inch or three-inch widths for medium-weight drapes.

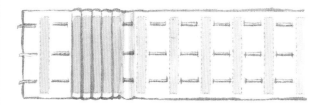

Velcro tape
Vertical bands of softened fibers between the gathering cords provide the soft surface for the hook side of Velcro to grip. A perfect solution for installing fixed valances.

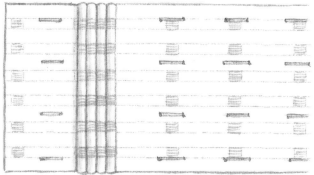

Deep pencil pleats
This six-inch-wide pencil-pleat heading tape is designed for longer, heavier curtains, quickly giving them a smart, professional look.

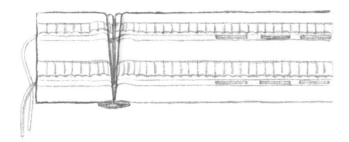

French or pinch pleats

Groups of three pleats lend curtains a smart, elegant look. This tape is already corded so the groups of three automatically gather up evenly across the curtain.

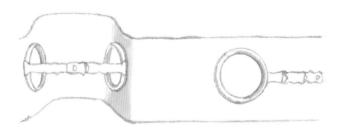

Large eyelet tape

A specialized tape for modern curtains with large eyelets to be threaded onto a rod. The tape allows eyelet rings to be attached to the top of the fabric.

Roman shade tape

This tape runs horizontally across Roman shades to create perfect folds. It also incorporates small pockets for the vertical pull-up cords to be threaded through.

Austrian shade tape

Fine, sheer tape that runs vertically down Austrian shades. The tape incorporates small rings through which the pull-up cords are fed.

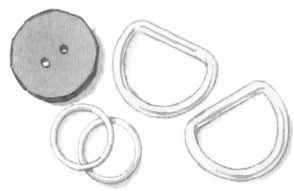

Curtain weights, small rings, and large D-rings

Use weights to neaten corners; stitch small rings to the back of shades for threading through the pull-up cords; and use D-rings on tiebacks.

INDEX

PHOTOGRAPHY CREDITS

The publisher would like to thank the following photographers for supplying the pictures in this book:

Page 1 Erica Lennard; **2** Frank Heckers; **3** Courtesy of *House Beautiful*; **4 top** Jeff McNamara; **4 bottom** Jeff McNamara; **5 top** Tim Beddow; **5 bottom** Toshi Otsuki; **6** Jonn Coolidge; **8** Steven Randazzo; **9** William Waldron; **10** Frank Heckers; **11** David Glomb; **12 left** William Waldron; **12 right** Fernando Bengoechea; **13** Dominique Vorillon; **16 top** Eric Boman; **16 bottom** Pierre Hussenot; **17** Jeff McNamara; **18 top** Courtesy of *House Beautiful*; **18 bottom** Courtesy of *House Beautiful*; **19 left** Peter Margonelli; **19 right** Jim Cooper; **20** Jeff McNamara; **21** Elizabeth Zeschin; **22 top** Toshi Otsuki; **22 bottom** Erica Lennard; **23** Toshi Otsuki; **25** Toshi Otsuki; **27** Gabi Zimmerman; **28** William P. Steele; **30** David Glomb; **31** Eric Boman; **32** Courtesy of *House Beautiful*; **33** David Montgomery; **34** Fritz von der Schulenburg; **35** Gordon Beall; **36** David Montgomery; **37 top** Jeff McNamara; **37 bottom** Courtesy of *House Beautiful*; **38** David Montgomery; **39** Gordon Beall; **40** James Merrell; **41** William Waldron; **42** David Prince; **43** Christopher Drake; **44 top** Richard Felber; **44 bottom** Jacques Dirand; **45** Courtesy of *House Beautiful*; **46** Jonn Coolidge; **47** Jeff McNamara; **48** Dana Gallagher; **49 top** Tom McWilliam; **49 bottom** Jonn Coolidge; **50** Toshi Otsuki; **51** Toshi Otsuki; **52** Michael Skott; **53 top** Steven Randazzo; **54** Paul Whicheloe; **55 top** Courtesy of *House Beautiful*; **55 bottom** Courtesy of *House Beautiful*; **56 left** Victoria Pearson; **56 right** Scott Frances; **57** Susan Gentry McWhinney; **58** Pierre Chanteau; **59** Christophe Dugied; **60** Jeff McNamara; **61 top** Steven Randazzo; **61 bottom** Michael Skott; **62 left** William Waldron; **62 right** William Waldron; **63** William Waldron; **64** Scott Frances; **66** Courtesy of *House Beautiful*; **67** David Glomb; **68** Fernando Bengoechea; **69** Peter Margonelli; **70** David Montgomery; **71 top** Jonn Coolidge; **71 bottom** Jeff McNamara; **72** Gordon Beall; **73** David Prince; **76–7** Joshua Sheldon; **78 left** David Montgomery; **78 right** Victoria Pearson; **79** Roger Davies; **82** Susan Gentry McWhinney; **84** Scott Frances; **86** Fernando Bengoechea; **87** Jeff McNamara; **88** Toshi Otsuki; **89 top** Toshi Otsuki; **89 bottom** Jim Hedrich; **90** Fernando Bengoechea; **92** Pia Tryde; **93** Courtesy of *House Beautiful*; **94** Steven Randazzo; **96** David Prince; **98** Erica Lennard; **99 top** Dana Gallagher; **99 bottom** Toshi Otsuki; **100 left** Gross & Daley; **100 right** Toshi Otsuki; **101** Tria Giovan; **104 left** Tom McWilliam; **104 right** Thibault Jeanson; **105** Fernando Bengoechea; **108–9** Joshua Sheldon; **110** Toshi Otsuki; **111 top** David Glomb; **111 bottom** Dominique Vorillon; **112 left** Courtesy of *House Beautiful*; **112 right** Courtesy of *House Beautiful*; **113** David Glomb; **116 top** Fernando Bengoechea; **116 bottom** Courtesy of *House Beautiful*; **117** Dominique Vorillon; **120–1** Joshua Sheldon; **122** Thibault Jeanson; **123** Tim Beddow; **126 left** Robert Lautman; **126 right** Tim Street-Porter; **127 top** Courtesy of *House Beautiful*; **127 bottom** Peter Margonelli; **130** Jeff McNamara; **131** Toshi Otsuki; **132** Thibault Jeanson; **133** Michael Skott; **134** David Glomb; **135 left** Toshi Otsuki; **135 right** Michael Skott; **136** David Glomb; **137 top** Scott Frances; **137 bottom** Jeremy Samuelson; **138 left** Peter Margonelli; **138 right** Gorgon Beall; **139 top** David Phelps; **139 bottom** Charlie Arber; **140 left** Tim Street-Porter; **140 right** Tria Giovan; **141** William Waldron; **142 bottom** Peter Margonelli; **142 top** Toshi Otsuki; **143** Fritz von der Schulenburg; **144** Jeff McNamara; **145** Christopher Drake; **146** Dominique Vorillon; **147** David Glomb; **148** Jonn Coolidge; **149** David Glomb; **150** Toshi Otsuki; **151** Steven Randazzo.